COACHING COMPETITIVE SPORTS

HOW TO DEVELOP AND ASSESS PLAYER KNOWLEDGE, SKILLS, AND INTANGIBLES

Tammy Heflebower | Logan Heflebower
with Dackri Davis

MARZANO
Resources

555 North Morton Street
Bloomington, IN 47404
888.849.0851
FAX: 866.801.1447

email: info@MarzanoResources.com
MarzanoResources.com

Visit **MarzanoResources.com/reproducibles** to download the free reproducibles in this book.

Printed in the United States of America

Library of Congress Cataloging-in-Publication Data

Names: Heflebower, Tammy, author. | Heflebower, Logan, author.
Title: Coaching competitive sports : a field book for assessing the
    intangibles / Tammy Heflebower, Logan Heflebower.
Description: Bloomington, IN : Marzano Resources, [2024] | Includes
    bibliographical references and index.
Identifiers: LCCN 2023019925 (print) | LCCN 2023019926 (ebook) | ISBN
    9781943360802 (paperback) | ISBN 9781943360819 (ebook)
Subjects: LCSH: Coaching (Athletics)
Classification: LCC GV711 .H45 2024 (print) | LCC GV711 (ebook) | DDC
    796.07/7--dc23/eng/20230711
LC record available at https://lccn.loc.gov/2023019925
LC ebook record available at https://lccn.loc.gov/2023019926

Solution Tree
Jeffrey C. Jones, CEO
Edmund M. Ackerman, President

Solution Tree Press
President and Publisher: Douglas M. Rife
Associate Publishers: Todd Brakke and Kendra Slayton
Editorial Director: Laurel Hecker
Art Director: Rian Anderson
Copy Chief: Jessi Finn
Production Editor: Paige Duke
Copy Editor: Evie Madsen
Proofreader: Elijah Oates
Text and Cover Designer: Julie Csizmadia
Acquisitions Editor: Hilary Goff
Assistant Acquisitions Editor: Elijah Oates
Content Development Specialist: Amy Rubenstein
Associate Editor: Sarah Ludwig
Editorial Assistant: Anne Marie Watkins

Acknowledgments

We would like to acknowledge the many great coaches we had along the way. You changed us. You made us better. For that, we are forever grateful.

—Tammy Heflebower, Logan Heflebower, and Dackri Davis

Marzano Resources would like to thank the following reviewers:

Doug Crowley
Assistant Principal
DeForest Area High School
DeForest, Wisconsin

Louis Lim
Principal
Bur Oak Secondary School
Markham, Ontario, Canada

Jennifer Steele
Assistant Director, Athletics and Activities
Fort Smith Public Schools
Fort Smith, Arkansas

Visit **MarzanoResources.com/reproducibles** to download the free reproducibles in this book.

Table of Contents

Reproducible pages are in italics.

ABOUT THE AUTHORS ix

CONTRIBUTING ATHLETES xi

INTRODUCTION 1

   Coaching Challenges 2

   Family Commitments and Demographics 3

   Pandemic Impact 6

   Tools for Effective Coaching 7

   About This Book 8

CHAPTER 1

ESTABLISH COACHING ROLES AND EXPECTATIONS   **11**

   Sport Coaching Defined 11

   Characteristics of Successful Coaches 13

   Coaching Roles and Expectations 19

   Summary 22

   Evaluating My Coaching Competencies 23

CHAPTER 2

FOSTER POSITIVE PLAYER-COACH RELATIONSHIPS	27

Child-Development Models 28
Implications for Coaches 36
Successful Player-Coach Relationships 43
Activities for Team Building 45
Summary 48
Implementing the Practice Cycle 49

CHAPTER 3

DETERMINE WHAT YOU WILL TEACH AND ASSESS	51

Proficiency-Based Coaching 52
Priority Knowledge, Skills, and Intangibles 54
Developmental Sports Scales 58
Summary 72
Planning Practice Sessions 73

CHAPTER 4

USE DEVELOPMENTAL SPORTS SCALES FOR TRACKING, FEEDBACK, AND GOAL SETTING	75

Team Expectations 75
Progress Tracking 79
Reflection Practices 85
Characteristics of Quality Feedback 88
Goal Setting 91
Summary 95
Setting SMART Goals 96

CHAPTER 5

CASE STUDY AND EXPERIENTIAL VIGNETTE OF COACH HEFLEBOWER'S PLAYERS	97

Collegiate Case Study 97
High School Experiential Vignette 107
Summary 112

EPILOGUE 113

APPENDIX A

GENERIC DEVELOPMENTAL SPORTS SCALE TEMPLATE   **115**

Sample Developmental Sports Scale Template 116

APPENDIX B

DEVELOPMENTAL SPORTS SCALES FOR BASEBALL   **117**

*Glove Positioning and Ball Handling Developmental
Sports Scale Template* 118

Eyes and Ball Tracking Developmental Sports Scale Template 119

Footwork and Range Developmental Sports Scale Template 120

APPENDIX C

DEVELOPMENTAL SPORTS SCALES FOR BASKETBALL   **121**

Defense Developmental Sports Scale Template 122

Ball Handling Developmental Sports Scale Template 123

Shooting Developmental Sports Scale Template 124

APPENDIX D

DEVELOPMENTAL SPORTS SCALES FOR FOOTBALL   **125**

Safety Developmental Sports Scale Template 126

Punter Developmental Sports Scale Template 127

Quarterback Developmental Sports Scale Template 128

APPENDIX E

DEVELOPMENTAL SPORTS SCALES FOR SOFTBALL   **129**

Pitching Accuracy Developmental Sports Scale Template 130

Pitching Velocity and Spin Developmental Sports Scale Template . . 131

Pitching Execution Developmental Sports Scale Template 132

APPENDIX F

DEVELOPMENTAL SPORTS SCALES FOR SOCCER   **133**

Ball Control Developmental Sports Scale Template 134

Passing Accuracy Developmental Sports Scale Template 135

Spatial Awareness Developmental Sports Scale Template 136

Strength and Power Developmental Sports Scale Template 137

Tactical Knowledge Developmental Sports Scale Template 138

APPENDIX G

DEVELOPMENTAL SPORTS SCALES FOR TRACK AND FIELD	139

Long Jump Developmental Sports Scale Template 140

Shot Put Developmental Sports Scale Template 141

400-Meter Dash Developmental Sports Scale Template 142

APPENDIX H

DEVELOPMENTAL SPORTS SCALES FOR VOLLEYBALL	143

Outside Hitter Attacking Developmental Sports Scale Template . . . 144

Blocking Developmental Sports Scale Template 145

Passing Developmental Sports Scale Template 146

APPENDIX I

DEVELOPMENTAL SPORTS SCALES FOR INTANGIBLES	147

Communication Developmental Sports Scale Template 148

Effort and Attitude Developmental Sports Scale Template 149

Coachability Developmental Sports Scale Template 150

Hustle Developmental Sports Scale Template 151

Teamwork Developmental Sports Scale Template 152

REFERENCES AND RESOURCES **153**

INDEX **159**

About the Authors

 **Tammy Heflebower, EdD,** is a highly sought-after school leader and consultant with vast experience in urban, rural, and suburban districts throughout the United States, Australia, Canada, Denmark, Great Britain, and the Netherlands. She has served as an award-winning classroom teacher, building leader, district leader, regional professional development director, and national and international trainer. She has also been an adjunct professor of curriculum, instruction, and assessment at several universities and a prominent member and leader of numerous statewide and national educational organizations.

Tammy was vice president and then senior scholar at Marzano Resources and continues to work as an author and associate with Marzano Resources and Solution Tree. In addition, she is the CEO of her own company, !nspire Consulting (https://inspirementor.com), specializing in powerful presentation and facilitation techniques, which she writes about and shares worldwide. Tammy is sole author of the *Presenting Perfected* book series and lead author of *Crafting Your Message: Tips and Tricks for Educators to Deliver Perfect Presentations*. She is also lead author of the best-selling, award-winning *A School Leader's Guide to Standards-Based Grading*, lead author of the award finalist *A Teacher's Guide to Standards-Based Learning*, and coauthor of *Collaborative Teams That Transform Schools: The Next Step in PLCs* and *Teaching & Assessing 21st Century Skills*. She is a contributing author to over a dozen other books and publications, many of which have been translated into multiple languages and are referenced internationally.

Tammy holds a bachelor of arts degree from Hastings College in Nebraska, where she was honored as Outstanding Young Alumna and her volleyball team was inducted into the athletic hall of fame. She also serves as a foundation trustee. Tammy has a master of arts from the University of Nebraska

Omaha and earned her educational administrative endorsement and doctorate from the University of Nebraska–Lincoln.

To book Tammy Heflebower for professional development, contact pd@SolutionTree.com.

Logan Heflebower has been coaching baseball since his collegiate playing career came to a close in 2019. He is the infield coach at Division II, Colorado Christian University, in Lakewood.

Logan was the head baseball coach at Weld Central High School in Keenesburg, Colorado, in 2022. During his time at Weld Central, he helped develop two first team all-conference players. Prior to coaching at the high school level, Logan was a private instructor for pre–high school baseball players at Diamond Club Baseball in 2020–2021.

During Logan's playing career at Division II Regis University from 2014–2019, he was a member of the RMAC in Denver, Colorado. He was a back-to-back Gold Glove Award winner at shortstop in 2017 and 2018. Logan was also a two-time All-RMAC second team nominee in 2018 and 2019, and a four-year academic All-RMAC Honor Roll student-athlete from 2016–2019. Logan remains a well-known name and face in the RMAC; he boasts the single season and career records for most assists and double plays in Regis Baseball history. Logan has a bachelor's degree in health and exercise science, and a master's degree in healthcare administration from Regis University.

Dackri Davis, PhD, is a high school principal in Denver, Colorado. Previously, she was director of college and career success for Aurora Public Schools. In this role, Dackri centered on graduation requirements, concurrent enrollment, Advanced Placement classes, International Baccalaureate programs, Individual Career and Academic Plans, and supporting all school counselors in the district. Prior to being a director, Dackri was a principal in Aurora and Denver, and an athletic director and high school history teacher for twelve years.

Dackri is passionate about supporting students to grow, succeed, and think critically. Being an associate with Marzano Resources allows her to share her knowledge and support to impact student achievement. She earned a bachelor's degree in history from Piedmont University in Demorest, Georgia, a master's degree in history from the University of West Georgia in Carrollton, and a principal licensure from Kennesaw State University in Kennesaw, Georgia. One of her proudest moments was earning her doctorate degree in educational policy studies focusing on race, class, and gender at Georgia State University in Atlanta.

Contributing Athletes

 **Mike Heflebower** is the owner and operator of Heflebower Funeral & Cremation Services (https://heflebowerfuneralservices.com) in Highlands Ranch, Colorado. He has over thirty-six years of funeral service experience in all facets of the industry and has served families in Colorado, Nebraska, and Kansas.

Mike is an alumnus of Hastings College in Nebraska, and a 1990 graduate of the Kansas City, Kansas School of Mortuary Science. He played football (free safety, punter, and kicker) at Hastings and was a three-sport athlete in high school, playing football and basketball, and running track. He earned numerous all-conference honors throughout his athletic career. Mike continued to play competitive volleyball, basketball, and softball after his collegiate athletic career. He is an avid snow skier, road biker, and hiker, continuing his passion for sports.

Over the years Mike volunteered as a special teams college football coach and coached football for years at his sons' middle school. He also volunteer-coached his sons in football, basketball, and baseball.

Nate Heflebower is a 2022 magna cum laude graduate from the University of Colorado Colorado Springs (UCCS). He was also a four-year student-athlete with the UCCS Baseball program. During his collegiate career, Nate was recognized as a two-time Rocky Mountain Athletic Conference (RMAC) All-Academic Honor Roll athlete. He was a part of two RMAC playoff appearances in 2021 and 2022, securing the Mountain Lions' first-ever conference championship title in 2021 as the starting second baseman, and first NCAA Division II Regional Tournament appearance.

During Nate's high school career, he was a member of Rock Canyon High School's 2017 and 2018 regional championship baseball teams, securing two Elite Eight appearances. Nate graduated from UCCS with a bachelor's degree in sports communication. He is the chief information officer of A Paws in Time (https://apawsntime.com), one of the Heflebower family businesses.

Taylor Wilpolt is a business analyst with experience in business development, corporate development, and investor relations. Taylor holds a bachelor of science degree in finance from the University of Colorado Colorado Springs (UCCS), where she was honored as a summa cum laude graduate. She was a four-year NCAA student-athlete on the UCCS Women's Soccer team. Her soccer team made the national tournament all four years and won the 2021 Rocky Mountain Athletic Conference (RMAC) Championship. Taylor was named the hardest worker as a freshman and was a member of the Captain & Leadership Council.

Cortney Heflebower is a highly qualified secondary mathematics teacher. Cortney holds a bachelor's degree in mathematics, with a minor in education. Cortney earned a master's degree in special education, with licensure to teach secondary mathematics, K–12 special education, K–12 culturally and linguistically diverse education, and elementary education. Cortney earned an advanced degree at Regis University in Denver, Colorado, where her lifelong aspirations of playing collegiate softball came to fruition. Cortney played all four years and was recognized as a three-year letter winner at Regis. She was also selected to the 2020 RMAC All-Academic Honor Roll, while simultaneously volunteering for a variety of softball lessons, camps, and clinics. Before competing at Regis, Cortney earned several high school all-state and all-conference awards as a pitcher and infielder.

Introduction

Did you dream of starting on your high school varsity soccer team as the leading scorer? Did you see yourself soaring through the air to dunk a basketball on your college team? Were you hoping to make it as a Gold Glove shortstop in the big leagues? These dreams are part of our motivation as coaches; they also fill the minds of the youth we coach. Many of these aspirations will come true—at least to some degree. Some will not. The key differences often lie with the caliber of coaches and their relational qualities athletes experience.

For most competitors, knowing what specifically to do to achieve in a sport is a mystery. Some players will labor hours in the driveway with parents pretending to be goalies; others will spend exorbitant amounts of hard-earned money attending every possible camp and obtaining private lessons; yet others hope their parents will contribute the most time and money to the school athletic club to garner their coach's favor. There are so many unwritten rules about *which coach wants what things*. They are not only head spinning but also heartbreaking at times.

Sports are a big part of the lives of many youth. School-sponsored sports run the gamut and are amazing in many ways. Sports are a vessel in which students can grow their physical and emotional capacity, learn key life lessons, find inspiration, gain experience working with peers, and develop relationships with coaches. Conversely, sports can harm some indefinitely, be the biggest disappointment, or proliferate the lives of many young people, their coaches, their schools, and their parents. They also provide unique opportunities for coaches to hone their craft, nurture players' abilities, and collaborate with parents.

This book aims to help sports coaches think and plan clearly to live the objectivity they claim and assist school-aged athletes to know what to do to become better in their sports. This resource will also more indirectly assist athletic directors in mitigating player-coach-parent issues and help parents better understand the expectations for their children's sports experiences. This resource could be not only career-changing for sports coaches but also life-changing for student-athletes.

Coaching Challenges

Despite the many rewards of their position, coaches encounter unique challenges. This is especially true for those coaches who are also teachers. In many states and provinces, you must be a practicing teacher to be a middle or high school competitive sports coach. Florida Memorial University associate professor Christopher Saffici (2015) wrote in *The Sport Journal*, "More than forty percent of all full-time secondary teachers have some type of coaching responsibility." Specifically, physical education teachers find a natural link to coaching. Saffici (2015) noted it's rare for a school to hire a candidate only to teach physical education; the teacher is almost always expected to coach.

Career data and information site CareerExplorer (n.d.) put the number of physical education teachers in the United States at 20,600, and projects job growth at over 9 percent through 2026. Not to mention the myriad of other middle and high school teachers who coach at least one sport, while some coach multiple sports. Additionally, there are more than 6.5 million youth sports coaches in the United States, and often teachers coach youth sports outside formalized middle and high school sporting teams (Aspen Institute, n.d.b). For instance, they may volunteer as their child's football coach, soccer assistant, or volleyball score-keeper. They are involved in youth sports but are often unpaid. When reviewing where youth regularly play sports, the number one location is on a school team (Sports & Fitness Industry Association, 2021).

While many effective teachers are also impressive coaches—directly connecting the knowledge and skills of child development with successful teaching and learning techniques to coaching their sports—not all are. Some inadvertently act as if the two are mutually exclusive, with little overlap in practices, approaches, and behaviors. Consequently, a teacher (who is also a coach) may rant, spew expletives, provide vague guidance, limit feedback and communication, and, over time, damage the player-coach relationships they would otherwise foster as classroom teachers. (Think Dr. Jekyll and Mr. Hyde, here.) Teachers who are also coaches are not necessarily predictable. We contend great teachers *should* make great coaches. And great coaches should (and often do) exemplify notable teacher behaviors.

Saffici (2015) identified four types of professionals found in many middle and high schools. They were: (1) coach, (2) coach-teacher, (3) teacher-coach, and (4) teacher. The *coach* has little interest in teaching but does so only to coach, living for practices and games, whereas the *coach-teacher* and *teacher-coach* each has interest in coaching as well as teaching. These two differed a bit: *coach-teachers* were coaches first, teachers second, seeing themselves as coaches who happen to also teach and identifying professionally as coaches. The *teacher-coaches* were teachers first, coaches second, seeing themselves as teachers who also happened to coach. The last type, *teachers*, were just that; they taught without any coaching responsibilities and identified only as teachers.

One thing these roles had in common was the dynamic nature of the positions. The International Council for Coaching Excellence and the Association of Summer Olympic International Federations (2012) noted:

> Coaches work with increasingly diverse populations and face heightening demands from their athletes, their athletes' parents, administrators and fans. Coaches are required to fulfill a variety of roles that may include educator, guide, sport psychologist and business manager. The professional area has placed a new emphasis on positive interaction and overall development of athletes rather than simply the win-loss record. There is greater accessibility to information and visibility to a larger community in the digital age. All of these factors make coaching both more exciting and taxing than ever before. (p. 4)

Because of this immense responsibility, coaches can and should improve and expand their capabilities to meet the needs of the athletes they serve. Additionally, schools and other entities that employ coaches owe them sufficient training, philosophical understandings, and practical resources to guide them in their immeasurable roles. This is important not just for coaches but also for parents, caregivers, and families, who make a sizable investment when encouraging a child to participate in school sports.

Family Commitments and Demographics

Families make a significant investment of resources for each child involved in youth sports. They include, but are not limited to, considerable expenses, time, availability for family and social functions, and physical and emotional health.

FINANCIAL AND TIME COMMITMENTS

Parents expend a great deal of time and financial resources for their children to participate in organized school or club sporting activities. *TIME* Magazine senior editor Sean Gregory (2017) reported at the high end of the curve, some families spend more than 10 percent of their total income on the combination of fees, travel, camps, equipment, and other ancillary expenses. In "How Kids' Sports Became a $15 Billion Industry," Gregory (2017) wrote:

> A volleyball dad from upstate New York spent $20,000 one year on his daughter's club team, including plenty on gas: up to four nights a week she commuted 2½ hours roundtrip for practice, not getting home until 11:30 p.m. . . . . Others hand their children over entirely. A family from Ottawa sent their 13-year-old to New Jersey for a year, to increase his ice time on the travel hockey circuit. . . . This summer, 10 boys from across the U.S. stayed with host families in order to play for a St. Louis–based travel baseball club.

Sports are a major commitment for many families. Not to mention they are turning into a $15.3 billion market for the youth sports industry—growing 55 percent since 2010 (Gregory, 2017). Canadians spend a great deal as well—upward of $1,000 annually per child (Solutions Research Group Consultants, 2014).

Not only is there a financial investment but also a time cost to families and athletes. Editorial director of The Aspen Institute's Sports & Society Program Jon Solomon (2023) reported on average, children spent 11.9 hours per week on their sport, with some sports more time-intensive than others. For instance, baseball required 13.4 hours per week, basketball 12.3 hours per week, and soccer 10.8 hours per week (Solomon, 2023). The most time-intensive sports include baseball and sports that are year-round, like gymnastics.

A 2016 study sought to determine how family financial investment affects children's experience in organized sports (Dunn, Dorsch, King, & Rothlisberger, 2016). Studying 163 parent-child pairs, the study found "an inverse association between family financial investment and child sport commitment, mediated by children's perceptions of parent pressure and sport enjoyment" (Dunn et al., 2016). Table I.1 illustrates the costs for families with children ages eight to eighteen who played organized sports, by sport.

Table I.1: Annual Costs for Families Participating in Team Sports

Sport	Annual Costs for Families
Lacrosse	$7,956
Hockey	$7,013
Baseball or Softball	$4,044
Football	$2,739
Soccer	$1,472
Basketball	$1,143

Source: Adapted from Dunn et al., 2016.

What about annual costs for families participating in individual sports? An Aspen Institute survey (2020) gleaned the following data from families of players ages six to eighteen.

- **Tennis:** $1,326
- **Martial Arts:** $1,271
- **Gymnastics:** $1,183
- **Bicycling:** $747
- **Swimming:** $754
- **Track and Field:** $549
- **Cross Country:** $339
- **Wrestling:** $329

The Heflebower family estimated the costs for two sons playing baseball in the state of Colorado from age twelve (although many players often start before age twelve) through college (ages twenty-two and twenty-three), including summer leagues; off-season club ball experiences; traveling costs to and from practices, games, and out-of-state tournaments; equipment; and medical care to total upward of $600,000.

Some parents think they will be rewarded for all this time and money by securing big scholarships for their children, but that is rarely the case. In fact, an athlete's odds of playing beyond high school are unlikely: 1 in 99 go on to play in NCAA Division I basketball, and 1 in 1,860 make it to the NBA; in soccer, 1 in 73 will play in Division I and 1 in 835 will play MLS; baseball is a bit better, with 1 in 73 going on to play in Division I and 1 in 764 will play MLB; and football comes in at 1 in 41 athletes going on to play in NCAA Division I and 1 in 603 making it to the NFL (Scholarship Stats.com, n.d.).

Given this level of investment, coaches must ensure the benefits outweigh the costs and risks to students and their families. If families are going to invest so much time and money, participation in sports must be seen as a positive experience for their children. A positive outcome is more likely when coaches communicate the knowledge, skills, and intangibles players need to be successful in their sport.

PHYSICAL AND EMOTIONAL STRAINS

Families not only pay financially but also reported increased risks to their children's physical and emotional health. The American Academy of Pediatrics reported athletes younger than eighteen years old who specialize in a sport were at increased risk of injury, burnout, and depression (as cited in Brenner, 2016). In addition, *The American Journal of Sports Medicine* noted athletes who participated in a primary sport for more than eight months during a calendar year risked overuse injuries independent of age and sex (as cited in Post, Trigsted, Riekena, Hetzel, McGuine, Brooks, et al., 2017). Coauthors Charles Ryan Dunn, Travis E. Dorsch, Michael Q. King, and Kevin J. Rothlisberger (2016) found the more money families spend on youth sports, the more pressure students feel. And the more pressure students feel, the less enjoyment and commitment they have for the sport. Sadly, many youths—even at the college level—remark, "The game is no longer fun" or "My coach made me hate the sport I used to love."

One great resource known as *Project Play* (www.projectplay.org) focused on the need to develop more community-based play experiences for young people. Many parents want their child to play in community-based or school sports—and not for the competition. The most important outcomes for parents included mental health, physical health, fun, social skills, and peer relationships:

> "Parents appear to really be valuing right now the physical, emotional and social benefits of sport," [Travis E.] Dorsch [study director of the parent survey and founding director of the Families in Sport Lab at Utah State University] said. "Without in-person school in some places, sport becomes a vehicle where kids can still hopefully get these benefits. I also think a lot of parents view healthy competition as an important part of sports, and through competition, you can gain all of these other benefits. I think sometimes we create a false dichotomy over desired outcomes. They're not mutually exclusive." (Aspen Institute, 2020)

Coaches played a key role in whether athletes access these benefits. Effective youth coaching helps build these necessary and requested skills, not to mention setting up students for success and empowering them to weather life's challenges.

Pandemic Impact

It's well known the COVID-19 pandemic affected student learning; but it also affected school sports. In one fell swoop, some athletes went from practicing upward of fifteen hours per week and traveling hundreds of miles to events to being isolated from their team and unable to play their sport. In fact, physical activity among youth fell and obesity increased, as did health challenges and suicide rates (Aspen Institute, n.d.d). As schools recovered from the pandemic, youth sports have had mixed resurgence. The Aspen Institute, Utah State University, and North Carolina State University conducted online surveys of youth sports parents in the United States in 2020. Sociodemographic groupings were based on the U.S. Census Bureau, as well as past research about families with one or more children actively participating in organized sports. Respondents had children between the ages of six and eighteen who played sports and were representative of all fifty states and Washington DC (Aspen Institute, n.d.d). Consider the following:

> Organized sports are starting to return for youth of all ages, though as of September [2020], they are still half as active as they were prior to the pandemic. Parents are more willing to let their children play, and to spend money to support those activities, despite increasing concerns about the risks of COVID-19 transmission as well as transportation and scheduling concerns with school starting up again. Meanwhile, a growing number of youth have no interest in returning to the primary sport they played pre-pandemic—nearly 3 in 10 now. (Aspen Institute, 2020)

The consequence of the pandemic was that virtually 30 percent of student-athletes lost interest in their sport! In some ways, the break provided student-athletes the opportunity to reflect and decide if the rewards and enjoyment were worth the costs in time and money. While these numbers may be disheartening, they call coaches and families to consider athletes' priorities and expectations when it comes to investing in sports:

> A very concerning number: 29% of parents reported their child is not interested in sports, up from 19% in June [2020] and 18% in May [2020]. Having three in 10 kids who previously played sports no longer interested should be a major red flag for the youth sports ecosystem.
>
> "That's a frightening number for the viability of the youth sports system, but also for the health outcomes coming down the pipeline for kids," Dorsch said. "I think it's really important that we acknowledge kids maybe don't want to go back to sports the way they were. This is our opportunity to create a new youth sport system that kids want to come back to so we can reach that 29%, which is a moving target. How do we reframe the experience, whether it's focusing on interpersonal coach-athlete features or health features or the competition itself? This looks like a real pivot point." (Aspen Institute, 2020)

Despite the pandemic's effect on how many students participated in sports, school sports will continue to play a key role in students' development. Research shows youth who are physically active do better in life: they are one-tenth less likely to be obese, have up to 40 percent higher test scores, engage in less-risky behavior (drugs, smoking, unprotected sex), and 15 percent are more likely to attend college, often have higher self-esteem, and ultimately earn 7 to 8 percent higher in annual earnings (Aspen Institute, n.d.d). A substantial number of students are longing for a different experience, and coaches have the opportunity to offer them a spot on the team.

Coaches are uniquely placed to address the challenges youth athletes face. When coaches understand athletes' physical, social, and emotional needs, they are empowered to bring out the best in their players. Throughout this resource, you'll encounter the characteristics effective coaches use to do this work and gain tools for setting up your programs, practices, and experiences accordingly. You have the power to ensure the athletes entrusted to you experience the positive effects of sports.

Tools for Effective Coaching

This book aims to fill a gaping hole in the sports coaching field—namely, helping competitive sports coaches identify, reference, and assess the knowledge and skills players need to excel in their sport as well as the perceived intangibles that make athletes successful. *Intangibles* are characteristics like coachability, effort and attitude, stamina, accepting constructive criticism, being a valuable teammate—things that aren't physically quantifiable and yet are equally necessary for athletes to thrive. Author and baseball psychology expert Geoff Miller (2012) answers the question, What are intangibles? in his book *Intangibles: Big-League Stories and Strategies for Winning the Mental Game—in Baseball and in Life*:

> Intangibles are such mental game factors as focus, confidence, commitment, intensity, discipline, character, and heart. They are typically called *intangibles* because they are difficult, if not impossible, to measure quantitatively and objectively. The term itself has become a pop-culture catchall phrase, used in sportscasts, in draft rooms, and on playing fields as an explanation for any effect not directly related to a physical act in sports.
>
> Intangibles become tangible when we measure them in ourselves. Each of us has felt the impact of confidence. Each knows the difference between being focused and being distracted. We have all heard the voice of doubt in our own minds; we all know how pressure can produce physical symptoms such as shortness of breath and sweaty palms. . . . by giving intangibles a human context, we can understand the role they play in each athlete's life. . . . And by focusing on the intangibles in ourselves, we can improve our performance on and off the field. (p. 7)

In this book, we aim to do just that: make the intangibles measurable so coaches know how to monitor players' progress and teach them to take ownership of their path toward proficiency regarding the knowledge, skills, and intangibles of their sport.

As noted in a comprehensive two-year Aspen Institute study (n.d.d), "School leaders must put in place a set of aligned strategies and tactics to bring that more robust model to life, tailored to the interests of its students and assets of its community." That is exactly what this resource offers—a process for getting a coach's expectations (often opaque and mysterious) on paper. It may help solve the common questions players ask of coaches, such as "Why am I not playing more?" and "What must I do to get better?" This book may also provide sound justification for both coaches and athletic directors when fielding questions or concerns from players and parents. This book fosters and yields a transparent and unbiased process as well as a more student-centered model.

About This Book

The primary audience for this book is grades 6–12 competitive sports coaches. Throughout the text, we offer advice for customizing the tools and resources to suit your particular situation. We also offer frequent opportunities for personal reflection about your thinking and practice.

Reflection

When you see this Reflection symbol, take time to pause and think about what you've read, contemplate how you currently operate in your role and how you wish to improve, and take notes in the space provided so you can capture your ideas for implementation. Review your notes regularly to check and improve your practice.

You'll also find developmental sports scales throughout the text, which enable players to self-reflect and set goals based on specific criteria they need to master the knowledge, skills, and intangibles of their sport. These scales not only help athletes know and understand expectations but also give them a voice with coaches and teammates.

This book contains five chapters and robust appendixes.

Chapter 1 lays a foundation for understanding coaching and the essential characteristics effective coaches exhibit, combined into a coaching cycle for reflection and growth.

Chapter 2 explores child-development models that inform how coaches relate to players' cognitive needs, stage of development, and motivational type. It includes a practice cycle, considerations for fostering positive player-coach relationships, and activities for team building.

Chapter 3 establishes expectations for standards-based coaching. It offers a process coaches can use to determine essential knowledge and skills their athletes need to thrive in their sport. Readers learn how to share that clarity with their coaching team and use it to plan their practice sessions.

Chapter 4 shows coaches how to use developmental sports scales early on to establish expectations with their team. Readers also learn how to use developmental sports scales to effectively track team progress, provide quality feedback, and help players set ambitious goals to improve their skills.

Chapter 5 details a case study of how Coach Logan Heflebower used this book's model in two coaching situations—one at the high school level, the other in college. It includes background information before detailing the case study's method, findings, and conclusions.

The appendixes provide developmental sports scales for seven sports: (1) baseball, (2) basketball, (3) football, (4) softball, (5) soccer, (6) track and field, and (7) volleyball. The final appendix offers a template coaches can use to assess intangible skills for most sports.

We envision coaches using this resource daily, dog-earing the corners, and referencing it before, during, and after practices. We also envision coaches sharing the developmental sports scales with their players and encouraging them to self-reflect on their progress, self-monitor their behavior, and set goals for increasing proficiency.

Youth sports need more direct attention regarding unbiased knowledge and skills paired with the coaching attributes of those who lead them. This resource helps bridge any explicit or implicit gaps in player-coach expectations, feedback, evaluation, and relationship building by providing practical ideas and clarified expectations. Our goal is to take the guesswork out of this complex endeavor to provide respectful, kind, and fair support and guidance to coaches undertaking such responsibilities. This resource is your playbook. Put down your whistle and get ready to learn, unlearn, and relearn some key aspects for bringing back both joy and inspiration to all those involved in youth sports.

CHAPTER 1

Establish Coaching Roles and Expectations

As youth athletes, our favorite coaches were the ones who cared about us as people first and foremost. They knew enough about us to playfully banter, push us harder than we thought possible, and celebrate our successes. Our coaches were consistent and didn't play obvious favorites. They also understood how best to motivate each player on our teams. Some of us only needed an occasional pat on the back to continue working hard. Others responded best to *tough love*—pushing, cajoling, and subtle appreciating. And some required more assertive motivation—the kind that gets your attention directly and emphatically. The key was our coaches worked hard to figure *us* out, as much as we worked to understand them. The relationships were two-sided. Our best coaches got all that *and* had respected winning programs too.

To work effectively with youth athletes, coaches must think about the many roles they play—often fluidly interchanging them. In this chapter, we define coaching, considering the many contexts coaches operate in. Then we explore ten characteristics of successful coaches. We share a coaching cycle we've found to be effective for developing the ten characteristics. Finally, we address the roles of various coaches on a program's staff and how these roles connect to athlete development.

Sport Coaching Defined

A coach's role depends on context. One colleague may coach another. Parents may coach their child through a challenging situation. In some educational settings, an instructional expert coaches a teacher. Sometimes a coach serves in a volunteer capacity. In most middle and high schools, a coach has a paid position, coaching a sport in addition to teaching in the classroom.

So, what does a coach do? How do we, the authors, define the role for the purposes of this book? We propose the following definition from the International Council for Coaching Excellence and Association of Summer Olympic International Federations (2012): "Coaching is a process of guided improvement and development in a single sport at identifiable stages of athlete development" (p. 12). This definition is right for this book because it embraces the complexity of the coaching role while highlighting the importance of guiding athletes' improvement and development.

Reflection

PAUSE FOR A MOMENT TO REFLECT ON THE FOLLOWING QUESTIONS.

* **How do you define _coaching_?**

_____

_____

_____

_____

_____

_____

* **How might your coaching team define _coaching_?**

_____

_____

_____

_____

_____

_____

* **How might athletes in your school define _coaching_?**

_____

_____

_____

_____

_____

_____

Characteristics of Successful Coaches

To be a successful coach, you must be knowledgeable about the sport, skilled in demonstrating key skills, possess emotional objectivity, model appropriate adult behaviors, be a great on-the-spot decision-maker and effective communicator, and be qualified through state and local agencies. The International Council for Coaching Excellence (2012) notes,

> A coach who instills a sense of discipline or who unifies a group for a common purpose is every bit as successful as the league title-winning coach. The challenge to maximize effectiveness with various groups of athletes and changing circumstances is part of the allure and richness of coaching. Because of the diversity of the role and contexts, the delivery of coaching and what is deemed successful will always be situation-specific (p. 12).

Ultimately, coaches each must define *success* for themselves. And yet, there are key characteristics successful coaches share. Consider the following ten competencies for effective coaching. Use the reproducible, "Evaluating My Coaching Competencies" (page 23) to evaluate how these characteristics show up in your coaching.

1. **Know the sport and model professionalism:** While many coaches have a strong history of playing or watching the sport they coach, this is not always the case. If this applies to you, become a student of your sport. Strive to understand the offenses, defenses, player positions, and the many intricate rules of the sport. Well-coached teams avoid procedural penalties that are often an indication of the coaches' failure to attend to a detail or rule. In addition to modeling excellence, set expectations of professionalism such as timeliness, integrity, and bringing your best to each practice and game. Holding yourself to a high standard sets high expectations for your staff and players.

   Model the behaviors you expect from your players. If you won't tolerate disrespect between players, then you must treat your players, staff members, rival teams, and officials with respect. There will be bad calls, setbacks, and disappointments, and how you outwardly deal with these issues models that behavior for your players. We have seen all too often coaches screaming at the umpires and referees. These coaches, in turn, will see their players do the same. Players take the lead from the head coach.

2. **Understand athlete maturation level:** Effective coaches understand how players develop through differing maturation levels. Just as compassionate parents understand their toddler's time in the "terrible twos" is a natural phase of development, coaches must anticipate their athletes move through phases of physical and emotional development that impact their performance. Your players' physical development inherently determines the strength, endurance, and flexibility they will display in practices and games. The same applies to players' emotional maturity.

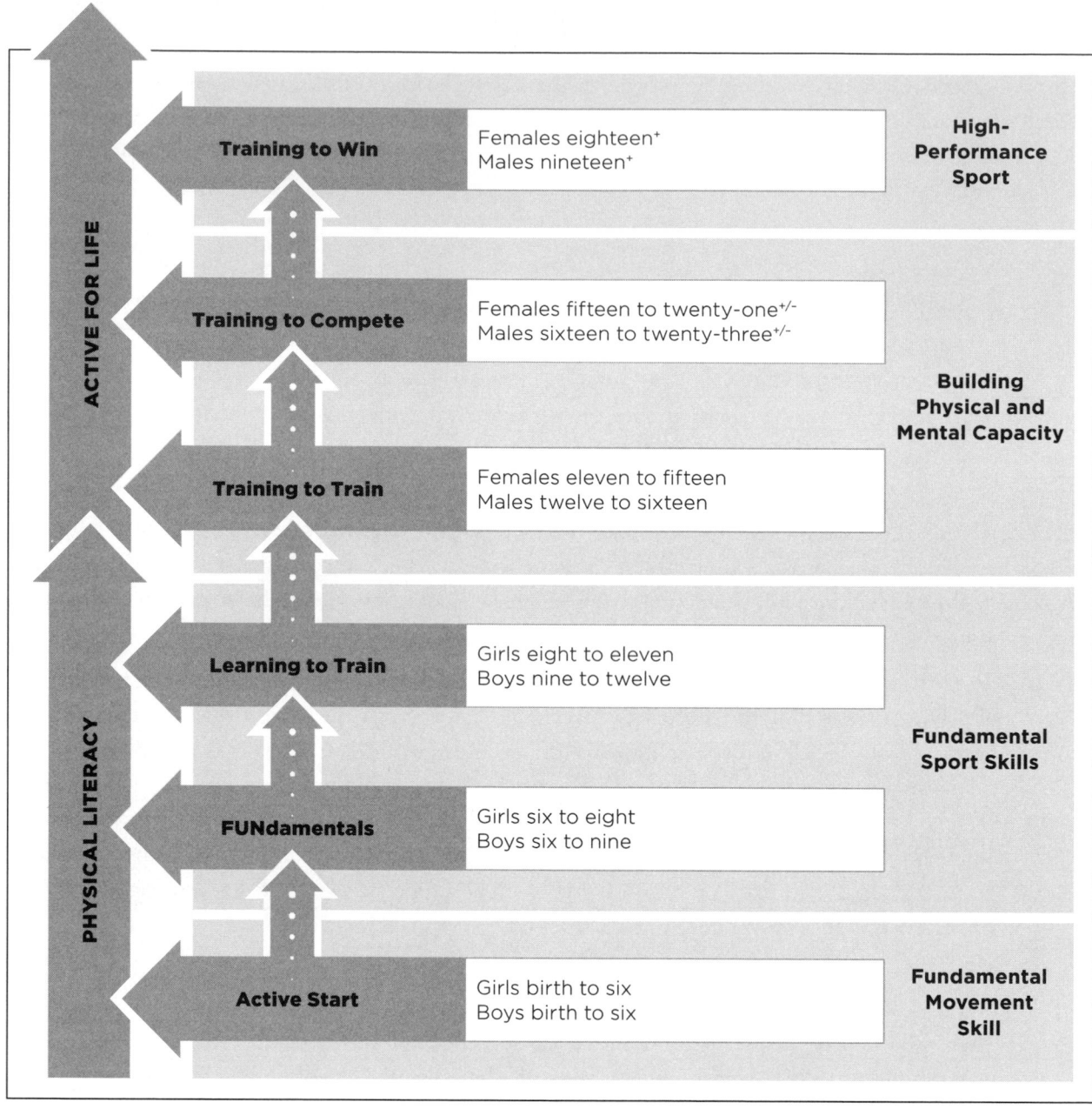

Figure 1.1: Long-term athlete development.

Coaches and sports experts Istvan Balyi and Ann Hamilton's (1995) foundational research showed children develop athletic skills differently based on their age. From birth to six years old, students are just beginning to practice physical activity; their focus should be on enjoyment rather than refining skills. By ages eight to twelve, youth are learning how to train for a sport, including learning practice drills and the nature of the sport to enhance skills. During the eleven to sixteen years old range, students can begin rigorous training to hone the essential mental and physical skills of their sport. From age fifteen to their early twenties, athletes fine-tune the skills they need for competition, such as making teams, gaining exposure, and moving into elite collegiate environments. Finally, the most elite athletes train to win. Figure 1.1 illustrates this progression.

Coaches may expand their understanding of athletes' development stages by studying child-development models (see chapter 2, page 28) and observing diverse groups of players at their level, as well as those above and below. This helps coaches better understand the maturation of athletes and have realistic expectations about the level of play and potential for improvement in the sport.

3. **Set the vision:** The coach creates a vision for the program based on the needs and stages of development of the athletes, and the organizational and social context of the program. The vision of the program lies with you and your support staff. What are your hopes for the program? Your players? This involves thinking deeply about your hopes for each individual player as well as the team collectively. Staff and players look to you to articulate this vision. Are you planning to win at all costs? Are you inclined to see improvement for each player as your end goal, letting the win-loss record take care of itself? Work at clarifying your vision until you can easily and consistently communicate it to your staff and players.

4. **Build relationships:** The successful coach builds positive and effective relationships with athletes and others associated with the program. Players are human. Coaches are human. Humans are social beings and thrive in relationships with others. Get to know each player. Know their families, the languages they speak at home, their backgrounds, and the nuances of their cultural expression. Care enough to banter with *all* of them, not simply a select few. Players notice all the implicit behaviors that feel friendly and fun. Remember life on a team isn't all business; make time for fun and connection! Establish routines and habits that encourage teammates to build relationships with one another and with your coaching staff. This might mean planning team-building activities that help players better understand one another; modeling how to encourage and celebrate one another; encouraging players when needed; and being vulnerable about yourself as a person when appropriate. In short, help your athletes see *your* human side.

5. **Communicate effectively:** Communicate often and effectively with players and their families, using various modes easily accessible for all (like group chats, phone applications, and website links). Effective coaches hold both formal and informal communication meetings to convey information, expectations, and progress. Additionally, make sure you have emergency contacts easily accessible. Highly effective coaches help families get to know one another as well. Provide a list of player names with corresponding jersey numbers, and parents' names to facilitate parent-to-parent communication and increased support of all players on your team. Parents don't cheer for players they don't know.

6. **Conduct effective practices:** Organize suitable and challenging practices for the athletes to nurture their development. Ensure the practice and performance environment is safe, conducive to the sport, well maintained, and fun. This includes attending to uniforms, equipment, and space; setting and maintaining standards of conduct between players; managing other coaches and support personnel like student managers; and making room for spontaneity and fun. Work toward aligning your practices to your players' needs rather than relying on mundane or rote practice drills. The developmental sports scales in this book (see chapter 3, page 58) help you to clearly identify players' strengths and needs so you can more easily determine the focus of your practices. You will be able to discern which areas of your sport need direct attention and

instruction to the whole team, a subgroup, or even a few individuals. This ensures you design practices at the appropriate level of challenge, provide specific help and support coinciding to individual players' needs, and identify the right next steps for your athletes. Such attention to specific needs helps players feel practices are interesting, emotionally safe, and less of a grind. Finally, adhere to beginning and ending times, which models integrity to staff and players as well as showing respect for players and their families.

7. **Structure impartial competitions:** Organize appropriate and challenging competitions for the athletes. Be aware of rival teams and their abilities, and prepare athletes for unique situations by carefully scouting upcoming opposing teams. Consider calling other coaches in the conference or using online tools such as Cloudscene (https://cloudscene.com), Statzon (https://statzon.com), and Wellspring (www.wellspring.com/products/scout) to help you prepare. Schedule all referees and umpires, and create and post game schedules well in advance. Additionally, be certain all travel and accommodation arrangements are made and communicated with athletes and parents.

8. **Make operational decisions:** The effective coach observes and responds to events appropriately, including all on- and off-field matters. For instance, you may need to address weather during an outdoor sporting event or deal with a player rule violation that occurred outside practices and games. Effective decision making is essential to fulfilling this function. Other teams may need to share your practice space. You may need to work around their practice needs and make other arrangements. You may have to make both planned and last-minute decisions like choosing a sick starter substitute or assistant coach. Prepare by thinking through a few contingencies with your coaching team *before* the need arises. Create a list of shared responsibilities or even a decision-making flowchart to help in your planning. Provide your coaches with safety plans for weather emergencies. Consider plans for addressing unruly fans or opposing coaches. Sometimes considering a few potential scenarios can help you make thoughtful preparations. For instance, "What will we do if we have a COVID outbreak on the team? Who might step in if the head coach has a medical emergency? How will we handle the needs of coaches' families alongside the needs of the team? Who can run the scoreboard if the scorekeeper doesn't arrive?" and so on.

9. **Monitor and ponder outcomes:** The coach evaluates the entire program as well as each practice and competition for areas of player strength and challenge. The coach reflects about the final win-loss record and what might have gone differently. Were there coaching errors made you need to address? Did coaches miss a key skill during practice? It is important to embed quality feedback and program evaluation from the athletes. How do the players feel? What have they learned? How have they gotten better? Create tools to evaluate program success based on factors like fun, diversity, participation, and retention rates, as well as competitiveness at your level (Aspen Institute, 2020).

10. **Set goals and improve:** The coach uses the reflections and evaluations to set specific goals and improve. Did the schedule include a grueling ending that you need to spread out better? Make that change. Did the team progress in its development and level of play? How do you know? Consider watching some videos of players early, midway, and toward the end of the season to note improvements. Set a goal for what you will start doing, keep doing, and stop doing. The coach also supports efforts to educate and develop other coaches. How will you provide positive

and corrective feedback to your coaching team? Did each fulfill your expectations? What specific strategies will you share? When is a good time to do this?

As we detail specific concepts that make a successful coach, it is important to note we generalize these concepts, so they may require variation depending on a specific role or coaching circumstance. Experienced coaches may be more proficient in exhibiting these functions, but all coaches should be about learning and growing throughout their tenure.

Figure 1.2 illustrates a cycle that encompasses these ten competencies. Note the categorizations of the competencies include learn, lead, execute, and adjust. We classified them for ease of reference. This cycle also helps coaches focus more specifically on improving identifiable coaching competencies for validation and improvement.

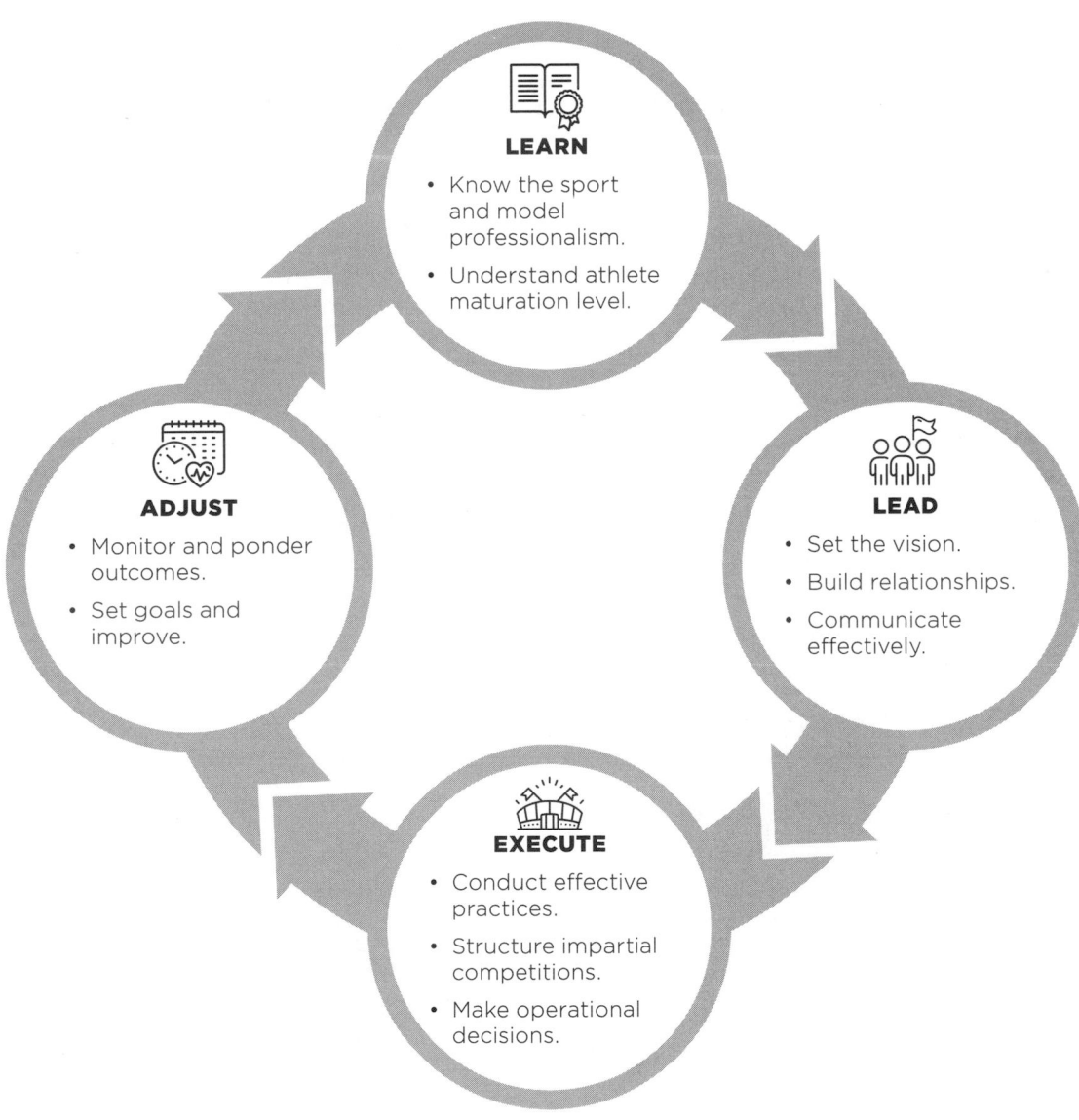

Figure 1.2: The cycle of coaching.

This cycle (see figure 1.2, page 17) helps coaches reflect on their strengths and challenges. Beginning with the Learn circle, ask yourself: "Is there anything more I need to learn about my sport or the psychology of working with youth athletes?" Next, focus on the Lead circle. What have you done for each of the competencies? What validates your practice? Where could you improve? As the cycle continues, consider how you are addressing the execution of the coaching competencies. For instance, are your practices efficient and effective? How do you know? Would others agree? Wrap up the cycle by considering the categories about reflection in the Adjust circle. Don't skip this step! If you want to improve, work at the details of your coaching practice. Consider keeping a copy of this cycle near you (in your office, or on your clipboard, tablet, or phone). Commit to reviewing the cycle once every couple of weeks. Use it with your coaching team and ask for feedback from others you trust and who can use the cycle as the basis for objective reflection.

Reflection

PAUSE FOR A MOMENT TO REFLECT ON THE FOLLOWING QUESTIONS.

* **How might you use the cycle of coaching to improve your approach?**

_____

_____

_____

_____

_____

_____

_____

* **Which aspect of the cycle is your strongest? Your weakest?**

_____

_____

_____

_____

_____

_____

_____

_____

❋ **How might you use it to set goals?**

_____

_____

_____

_____

_____

_____

Coaching Roles and Expectations

There are various coaching roles within a coaching team. Some programs have few coaches, others a plethora of them. Some programs have one head coach and an arsenal of volunteers. Others may have a head coach with a variety of specialized assistant coaches. No matter the number, clarifying each coach's role is important so the program runs efficiently.

The International Council for Coaching Excellence and Association of Summer Olympic International Federations (2012) defines various coaching roles such as head coach, advanced or senior coach, coach, and coaching assistants. In this book, we focus on three main roles: (1) head coach, (2) assistant coach, and (3) volunteer coach. In most settings, the head coach and assistant coach operate in paid positions (extra-duty payment schedules or stipends). Volunteers do not receive financial compensation.

Table 1.1 provides an overview of these positions as well as their roles and responsibilities.

Table 1.1: Coaching Roles and Responsibilities

	Head Coach	Assistant Coach	Volunteer Coach
Time Commitment	The head coach commits to: • Attending all games and practices	The assistant coach commits to: • Attending all games and practices	The volunteer coach commits to: • Attending most games and practices, depending on personal obligations
Responsibilities	The head coach is responsible for: • Planning, leading, and evaluating practices and competitions with input from coaching team • Overseeing the entire structure of the program • Recruiting (as applicable) • Hiring the coaching team • Supervising volunteers and assistants	The assistant coach is responsible for: • Planning and leading some portions of practices and competitions • Sharing direct input regarding the structure of the program • Supporting the head coach in recruiting (as applicable) • Providing volunteer coaches with guidance and support	The volunteer coach may be responsible for: • Planning or leading some portion of practices and competitions • Sharing input regarding the structure of the program

continued →

	Head Coach	Assistant Coach	Volunteer Coach
Sport Knowledge	The head coach is responsible for: • Having broad knowledge of the sport, rules, and positions • Regularly synthesizing skills and positions for most, if not all, players	The assistant coach is responsible for: • Having broad knowledge of the sport, rules, and positions • Having specific and extensive knowledge and skills in specialized areas • Synthesizing skills and positions for specific areas	The volunteer coach is responsible for: • Having basic knowledge of the sport, with some area of specialization
Sport Competencies	The head coach is responsible for: • Maintaining a wide spectrum of coaching functions in ever-changing practice and competition environments	The assistant coach is responsible for: • Maintaining specialized and practical competencies in ever-changing practice and competition environments	The volunteer coach may be responsible for: • Maintaining some specialized competencies in a structured environment • Providing limited support during competitions
Data and Evaluation	The head coach is responsible for: • Carrying out all-encompassing evaluation of results, research about the sport, and varying criteria • Making decisions about circumstances based on statistics and other information	The assistant coach is responsible for: • Collecting statistics and collating them for the head coach • Evaluating results using varying criteria • Helping make decisions about circumstances based on information	The volunteer coach may be responsible for: • Collecting statistics and collating a limited scope for the team • Evaluating results and varying criteria • Helping make decisions about circumstances based on information the head or assistant coach asks
Game-Day Responsibilities	The head coach is responsible for: • Making major decisions • Working directly with officials • Providing game-day lineups and making substitutions	The assistant coach is responsible for: • Making minor decisions • Providing input toward game-day lineups and substitutions • Focusing on a specific area of the game • Reviewing the opposing team for timely modifications and adjustments	The volunteer coach may be responsible for: • Making minor decisions • Providing input toward game-day lineups and substitutions • Focusing on a different specific area of the game • Reviewing the opposing team for timely modifications and adjustments

Source: Adapted from the International Council for Coaching Excellence & Association of Summer Olympic International Federations, 2012.

Given that each team's staff are unique, it's best to personalize these roles to your specific situation. Providing appropriate guidance to staff who fill various coaching positions in your program can help delineate roles and responsibilities during practices and competitions. Consider the strengths your coaches each bring to your team and allow them to take over responsibilities that align with these strengths. Maybe one coach has a knack for tracking statistics and creating graphics for the team to review. Another might be exceptional at motivating specific players with unique struggles.

This might look like putting the infield specialty coach in charge of opposing batter tendencies during a baseball game. The coach tracks where each batter is hitting and any nuances surrounding the batter's approach to make any necessary defensive shifts. Another example might be that your assistant volleyball coach keeps track of time-outs and notes defensive gaps. That way, during time-outs, that coach can provide input.

Reflection

PAUSE FOR A MOMENT TO REFLECT ON THE FOLLOWING QUESTIONS.

✳ **What are the various coaching roles on your staff?**

_____

_____

_____

_____

_____

_____

_____

_____

✳ **How do the roles and responsibilities within your program align with the roles and competencies chart (see the reproducible, "Evaluating My Coaching Competencies," page 23)?**

_____

_____

_____

_____

_____

_____

_____

✳ **What steps will you take to clarify staff roles and ensure you work together as an efficient and cohesive team?**

_____

_____

_____

_____

_____

_____

_____

_____

_____

Summary

Being a successful coach takes a great deal of deliberate learning, leading, executing, and adjusting! In this chapter, you encountered our definition of _coaching_, considered the many contexts coaches operate in, and had the chance to define what coaching means in your specific context. You encountered ten competencies effective coaches share as well as a coaching cycle you can use to monitor your growth toward mastering these competencies. At the end of the chapter, you explored various roles in most coaching programs, had the chance to reflect on who fills those roles on your team, and considered how you might work together as a more cohesive whole.

Evaluating My Coaching Competencies

Use the following chart to review the ten competencies of effective coaches. Read each statement and indicate your strength in each characteristic on a scale of 1 (weak) to 4 (strong). Finally, consider the reflection questions and write your response in the space provided, considering how you might shift your actions, habits, and routines to grow in future seasons.

Characteristics	Reflection Questions	Notes
Competency: Know the sport and model professionalism.		
I have a deep and nuanced understanding of the sport I'm coaching. ① ② ③ ④ I model professionalism for my staff and players. ① ② ③ ④ I treat staff and players with respect and expect them to do the same. ① ② ③ ④ I respond to setbacks and disappointments with integrity and expect others to do the same. ① ② ③ ④	• "What steps should I take to become more expert at the sport I'm coaching?" • "Is the practice environment safe and equipment in good condition?" • "What behavioral norms do I model well for staff and players? Where is there room for improvement?"	
Competency: Understand athlete maturation level.		
I understand players' development stages. ① ② ③ ④ I hold realistic expectations for players' physical and emotional capacities. ① ② ③ ④ I am aware of child-development models and their implications for players. ① ② ③ ④	• "How much information can players handle at their current stage of development?" • "How do my athletes' maturity levels affect their physical and emotional capacities?" • "How will I adjust my expectations in light of this information?"	
Competency: Set the vision.		
I have a robust vision for my players individually and our team collectively. ① ② ③ ④ I actively dream about where we can go as a team and what we can accomplish in the program. ① ② ③ ④ I frequently and effectively communicate this vision to staff, players, and families. ① ② ③ ④	• "What do I hope for my program?" • "What steps will I take to communicate my vision more clearly to my staff, players, and families?"	

page 1 of 3

Characteristics	Reflection Questions	Notes
Competency: Build relationships.		
I'm actively building positive relationships with all players. ①———②———③———④ I see my staff and players as human beings and respect their unique personalities and cultural expressions. ①———②———③———④ I build habits and routines that allow time for connection and fun. ①———②———③———④	• "What habits and practices do I use for building relationships with my players?" • "Do I build relationships objectively, or do I show favoritism?" • "What are my next steps in making authentic connections with players and their families?"	
Competency: Communicate effectively.		
I communicate frequently and efficiently with players and families. ①———②———③———④ I communicate in ways that are available to all members of the team. ①———②———③———④ I foster methods for two-way communication and invite feedback to optimize our program. ①———②———③———④	• "What methods do I use for communicating with players and their families?" • "How can I make communication efforts easy and effective for everyone?" • "Is communication two-way, consistent, and effective? If not, how will I take steps to improve communications among the team?"	
Competency: Conduct effective practices.		
I organize challenging practices for the team. ①———②———③———④ I adjust practice to respond to the unique needs of each player individually and the team as a whole. ①———②———③———④ I ensure the practice environment is physically and emotionally safe. ①———②———③———④ I ensure the equipment is in working order. ①———②———③———④ I begin and end practice on time. ①———②———③———④	• "Do I have a practice schedule and agenda?" • "Are practices rigid or flexible enough to respond to players' needs?" • "What steps will I take to make practice more effective for players individually and the team as a whole?"	
Competency: Structure impartial competitions.		
I am aware of rival teams' abilities and prepare the team to anticipate them. ①———②———③———④ I secure umpires and referees in a timely manner. ①———②———③———④ I ensure all players have transportation to competitions. ①———②———③———④	• "Will I scout other teams? How and when?" • "How and when will I secure umpires and referees?" • "What is my backup plan for staff, players, or officials who don't show?" • "How will athletes get to and from competitions? Do school parameters allow athletes to ride with parents?"	

Characteristics	Reflection Questions	Notes
Competency: Make operational decisions.		
I have contingency plans for sick staff, players, and officials. ① —— ② —— ③ —— ④ I respond to challenges with maturity and integrity. ① —— ② —— ③ —— ④ I know how to regulate my emotions under pressure. ① —— ② —— ③ —— ④ I make decisions that align with my goals and values. ① —— ② —— ③ —— ④	• "What are my contingency plans for weather, sick athletes or staff members, and other unexpected situations?" • "Do I respond to challenges or changed plans in a way that models maturity to players? If not, how will I work to change my response?"	
Competency: Monitor and ponder outcomes.		
I know this season's win-loss record and I evaluate my expectations based on that data. ① —— ② —— ③ —— ④ I ponder my actions, habits, and practices in light of the team's performance. ① —— ② —— ③ —— ④ I monitor players' development over the course of the season and use the data to make adjustments to the program. ① —— ② —— ③ —— ④	• "What is our win-loss record? How does that align with my expectations?" • "How have my actions contributed to our record?" • "Have I made errors in judgment?" • "How have players developed over time? How am I monitoring that development?"	
Competency: Set goals and improve.		
I evaluate my program, practices, and competitions to identify strengths and weaknesses. ① —— ② —— ③ —— ④ I consistently strive to grow myself, my staff, and my team to our full potential. ① —— ② —— ③ —— ④ I have structures in place to invite and receive feedback from staff, players, and families. ① —— ② —— ③ —— ④ I collaborate with staff, players, and families to improve our program. ① —— ② —— ③ —— ④	• "What were our team's strengths and weaknesses in this year's matches or games?" • "What will I do differently before next season?" • "How will I strive to grow in response to my observations of this season's performance?" • "How will I track my goals?"	

CHAPTER 2

Foster Positive Player-Coach Relationships

Some teams seem easier to coach than others. Why is that? You might wonder, "Why does it seem some of my players are so distracted? Why is this group so different from last year's team? Why can't I just get through to these couple of players? How can middle school athletes be *so different* from high school athletes? Why do some players continue to make the same mistakes? How can I help my team improve its focus when players are pulled in so many different directions? How can some players care too much and others too little? How do I motivate players whose priorities are so different? Why do some athletes respond so easily to direction while others need repeated instructions?"

The key to understanding these challenges lies in understanding athletes' mental and physical development. Coaching requires acute attention to many aspects, but it must include the brain *and* the body. The Aspen Institute (n.d.e) notes:

> Other countries recognize the value of trained coaches in growing participation. In the United Kingdom, the youth-coaching culture has been transformed through the introduction of a training framework. . . . The minimum ask: training in 1) coaching philosophy on how to work with kids, 2) best practices in the areas of physical literacy and sport skills, and 3) basic safety. (p. 24)

Better understanding in these areas will help coaches answer some of these questions and increase their skills as a sport coach.

In this chapter, we consider child-development models and how they inform the coach's relationship to athletes' cognitive development, hierarchy of needs, and motivational type. We explore the implications for coaches, such as constructing a practice cycle, considering players' needs, and boosting internal motivation. We also include considerations for fostering player-coach relationships and activities for team building.

Child-Development Models

The key to the body is through the brain. You read in the ten competencies (see chapter 1, page 13) that effective coaches understand how human development influences players' physical and emotional capacity. When coaches learn to recognize and respect players' stages of development—understanding the advantages and challenges of the stage they're in—those coaches can work *with* rather than against students' cognitive development.

Consider the following common instances.

- A seven-year-old player cares more about the dandelion in the outfield than the batter in the box.

- The coach raises her voice toward a middle school athlete, and the player responds by completely falling apart during the next drill.

- The assistant coach demonstrates the proper arm platform to pass a volleyball only to notice some of the players can't transfer the movement to their own arms.

Moments like these can leave coaches feeling frustrated, disappointed, or confused. But when they understand the stages of development players go through and practice seeing them through the lens of development and emotional maturation, they gain insight on players' surprising behaviors and can adjust processes for teaching skills, providing effective feedback, and monitoring expectations.

There are many insightful child-development theories available for study, including psychologist Erik H. Erikson's (1950) psychosocial developmental theory, psychoanalyst John Bowlby's (1983) attachment theory, psychologist Albert Bandura's (1977) social learning theory, and Swiss psychologist Jean Piaget's (1951) cognitive-development theory. For the scope of this book, we turn to the works of Piaget (1951), psychologist Abraham H. Maslow (1943, 1954, 1969, 1979), and professors Edward L. Deci and Richard M. Ryan (1985, 2008), to extrapolate the implications for a coach's work with players.

Reflection

✳ **What's your current level of understanding of child-development models?**

_____

_____

_____

_____

_____

_____

✳ **How have you seen child-development theory at work with athletes and coaches in the past?**

_____

_____

_____

_____

_____

_____

✳ **How does child-development theory currently inform your work with athletes?**

_____

_____

_____

_____

_____

_____

_____

PIAGET'S THEORY OF COGNITIVE DEVELOPMENT

Piaget's (1951) psychology model has contributed a great deal to the collective understanding of children's cognitive development at varying ages and stages (as cited in Papalia & Feldman, 2011; Waite-Stupiansky, 2017). Based on observations and clinical interviews, Piaget (1951) monitored how children approached various conceptual ideas and when and how they could think logically and draw valid conclusions. Piaget's (1951) theory said that a child develops through various stages before arriving at the stage of thinking like an adult. Specifically, Piaget (1951) monitored how children considered the idea of time, number, justice, and quantity. His theory of development purported that early childhood intellectual growth arises from interactions with objects in the environment, increasing in sophistication as children learn to deal with future situations (Piaget, 1951).

Educators Diane E. Papalia and Ruth Duskin Feldman (2011) summarized the theory's key implications: children are not born with the same types of cognitive processes as adults; rather, their processes tend to develop over time, as a response to their environment, and as they are exposed to new information. From this understanding, Piaget (1951) formed his theory of the four stages of cognitive development.

1. **Sensorimotor stage (birth to two years old):** During this stage, children engage in the first phase of cognitive development; they are learning about their environment through their senses. Their behaviors get gradually more goal oriented and purposeful (as cited in Nortje, 2021).

2. **Preoperational stage (two to seven years old):** During these years, children begin to use more mental abstractions. They engage in pretend play and can talk about previous events or people not in the room with them. They also begin to understand causality and categorization. They can sort and classify objects and people by similarities and differences, as well as understand more about quantities (fewer, more, smaller, bigger). They struggle with various dimensions and cannot easily reverse action steps. It is important to note they are still best at understanding their own perspective and viewpoint instead of those of others (as cited in Nortje, 2021). Therefore, rationalizing with children in this stage about how someone else feels or does something is difficult.

3. **Concrete operational stage (seven to eleven years old):** This stage begins at or near seven years of age. During these years, children are more capable of solving problems because they can consider other options, outcomes, and perspectives. They can perform more complicated mathematical operations, and their spatial abilities are better. They can estimate time and distance, as well as read a map and navigate and reverse the order or steps of an action (as cited in Nortje, 2021). These skills are increasingly important when teaching a sport.

4. **Formal operational stage (eleven years old through adulthood):** This final stage begins around age eleven. At this stage, children can consider more abstractions and hypothetical situations. They can consider multiple possibilities. They tend to apply reasoning more easily.

These stages offer insight into how to explain differences in children's behavior, motives, and values. Understanding these stages allows coaches to form accurate expectations for players based on their physical and cognitive maturity. Piaget's (1951) research formalized what many coaches experience with student-athletes on a daily basis: holding developmentally appropriate expectations for players is key to their success (and the coaches' peace of mind)!

Reflection

✳ **Did you know about the stages of Piaget's (1951) cognitive development theory before reading this chapter?**

_____

_____

_____

_____

_____

_____

✳ **What stage are most of your athletes currently in?**

_____

_____

_____

_____

_____

_____

✳ **What implications does this have for you as a coach?**

_____

_____

_____

_____

_____

_____

_____

MASLOW'S HIERARCHY OF NEEDS

Maslow (1943, 1954) is well-known in education for his theory of human motivation and the creation of his hierarchy of needs. This hierarchy originally had five needs: (1) physiology, (2) safety, (3) belonging, (4) esteem within a community, and (5) self-actualization. In later writings, Maslow (1969, 1979) included a sixth level: connection to something greater than self (as cited in Koltko-Rivera, 2006). Maslow (1943, 1954, 1969, 1979) purported that humans typically meet these needs in order, building from the lowest level to the highest. Figure 2.1 illustrates Maslow's (1943, 1954, 1969, 1979) model.

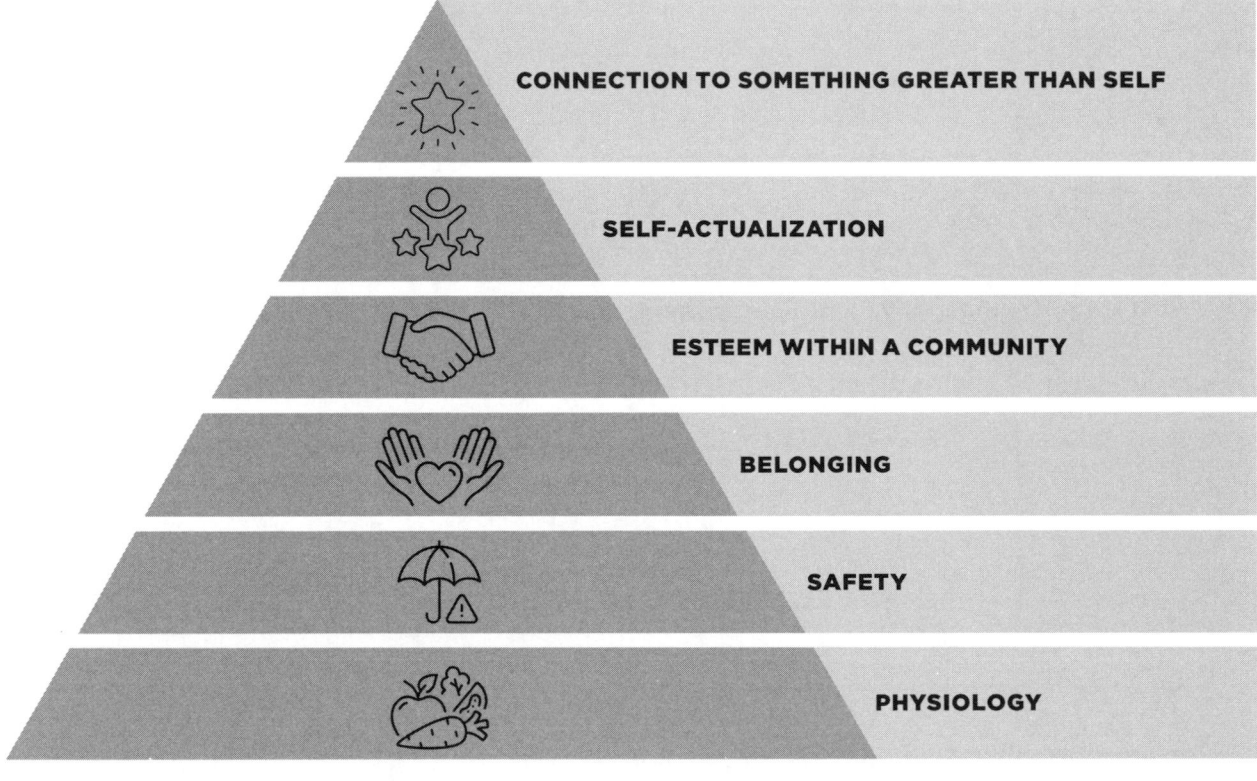

Source: Adapted from Maslow, 1943, 1954, 1969, 1979.

Figure 2.1: Maslow's hierarchy of needs.

Maslow's (1943, 1954) hierarchy of needs had a pyramid shape, with basic needs at the bottom of the pyramid and more high-level, intangible needs at the top. People can only move up to addressing their higher-level needs when their basic needs are adequately fulfilled. Consider the needs included at each of the following levels.

- **Physiology:** The most essential needs for human life are survival needs, including food and water, sufficient rest, clothing and shelter, overall health, and reproduction.

- **Safety:** Next among the lower-level needs is safety. Safety needs include protection from violence and theft, emotional stability and well-being, and health and financial security. Just like the physiological needs, safety is paramount.

- **Belonging:** The social needs on the third level of Maslow's (1943) hierarchy relate to human interaction and are the last of the so-called *lower needs*. Among these needs are friendships and family bonds—both with biological family (parents, siblings, and children) and chosen family (spouses and partners). Physical and emotional bonds are important to achieving a feeling of elevated association.

- **Esteem within a community:** The *higher needs*, beginning with esteem, are ego-driven needs. The primary elements of esteem are *self-respect* (the belief that you are valuable and deserving of dignity) and *self-esteem* (confidence in your potential for personal growth and accomplishments). Maslow (1943) specifically noted self-esteem can be broken into two types: (1) esteem based on respect and acknowledgment from others, and (2) esteem based on one's own self-assessment. Self-confidence and independence stem from this latter type of self-esteem.

- **Self-actualization:** *Self-actualization* describes the fulfillment of a person's ultimate potential. These needs include education, skill development (the refining of talents in areas such as music, athletics, design, cooking, and gardening), and broader goals like learning a new language, traveling to new places, and winning awards. At this level, people seek to fulfill their highest potential.

- **Connection to something greater than self:** This sixth level was not included in Maslow's (1943, 1954) original hierarchy of needs. However, in later writings, Maslow (1969, 1979) recognized that the pinnacle of personal fulfillment occurs when a person *transcends the self*—meaning the person longs to fulfill a higher purpose by helping *others* move up the hierarchy of needs.

Maslow (1943, 1951, 1969, 1979) said in essence that for some people, needs may appear in a different order or be absent altogether. People may feel a mix of needs from different levels at any given time, and they might vary in degree (Maslow, 1954). He contributed the idea that internal needs and motivations, not simply external rewards, influence behaviors (Maslow, 1954).

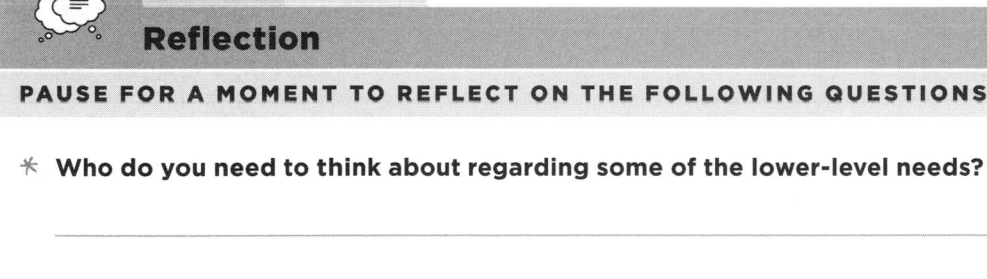

Reflection

PAUSE FOR A MOMENT TO REFLECT ON THE FOLLOWING QUESTIONS.

✳ **Who do you need to think about regarding some of the lower-level needs?**

_____

_____

_____

_____

_____

✳ **How might you pay closer attention to players' needs?**

_____
_____
_____
_____
_____
_____

✳ **How might this understanding of human needs help your team be more successful?**

_____
_____
_____
_____
_____
_____
_____
_____
_____

DECI AND RYAN'S SELF-DETERMINATION THEORY

The work of Deci and Ryan (2008) centered on motivation—in particular, types of motivation as predictors of performance outcomes. Deci and Ryan's (2008) research posited an empirically based theory of human motivation, development, and wellness called _self-determination theory (SDT)_. When applied to physical activity, sport, and health, SDT distinguished intrinsic and extrinsic motivations. _Intrinsic motivation_ caused participation in an activity because of the inherent pleasure the activity itself provides, whereas _extrinsic motivation_ caused participation in an activity to obtain a more tangible reward or recognition, or to avoid punishment (Ryan, Williams, Patrick, & Deci, 2009). In short, coaches want players to participate because they _want to_, not because they _have to_.

Intrinsic and extrinsic motivation theories the SDT describes have implications for how coaches motivate athletes: "Events that are perceived to negatively impact a person's experience of autonomy or competence will diminish intrinsic motivation, whereas events that support feelings of autonomy and competence will enhance intrinsic motivation" (Ryan et al., 2009, p. 110). When athletes know what they are expected to do, they experience a sense of _autonomy_—the feeling they are in control of what happens to them. This simple practice increased the likelihood of players operating from more intrinsic than extrinsic motivation. What does extrinsic motivation look like? Ryan and colleagues (2009) explain:

While a given sport activity may be highly interesting to an individual, a controlling coach who pressures and orders about his or her players can easily diminish a person's interest and joy of engagement. Similarly, conditions in which one faces non-optimal, overwhelming challenges can lead to feeling incompetent and to disengage. (p. 110)

So, what motivates youth athletes? A 2014 George Washington University study provided interesting results. The study showed nine of ten students reported *fun* as the main reason they participate in sports. In fact, those surveyed gave eighty-one reasons for participating, and *winning* was number forty-eight on the list (as cited in Visek, Achrati, Mannix, McDonnell, Harris, & DiPietro, 2015)! Students reported they wanted a place to try to do their best, and they wanted to know the score, but most didn't obsess over the actual results—they moved on minutes after the game ended (Active Network & Sporting Goods Manufacturers Association, 2012). There may be some misalignment between what students say they want (fun) and what parents or coaches may want (wins). Youth quit sports because they lose interest (Active Network & Sporting Goods Manufacturers Association, 2012). When coaches listen to what athletes say about their goals for sports, coaches can better align their vision with the athletes, especially during the early formative years when youth are learning a sport. Athletes come with varied abilities, interests, and goals. At the middle and high school levels, coaches should strive to have opportunities for the variations in athletes. Many of them will not go on to play at the college or professional level, so rethinking your purposes may be warranted. "We envision schools in which all students have the opportunity to develop through sports the educational, social, emotional and physical benefits that will serve them in life" (Aspen Institute, n.d.d, p. 3).

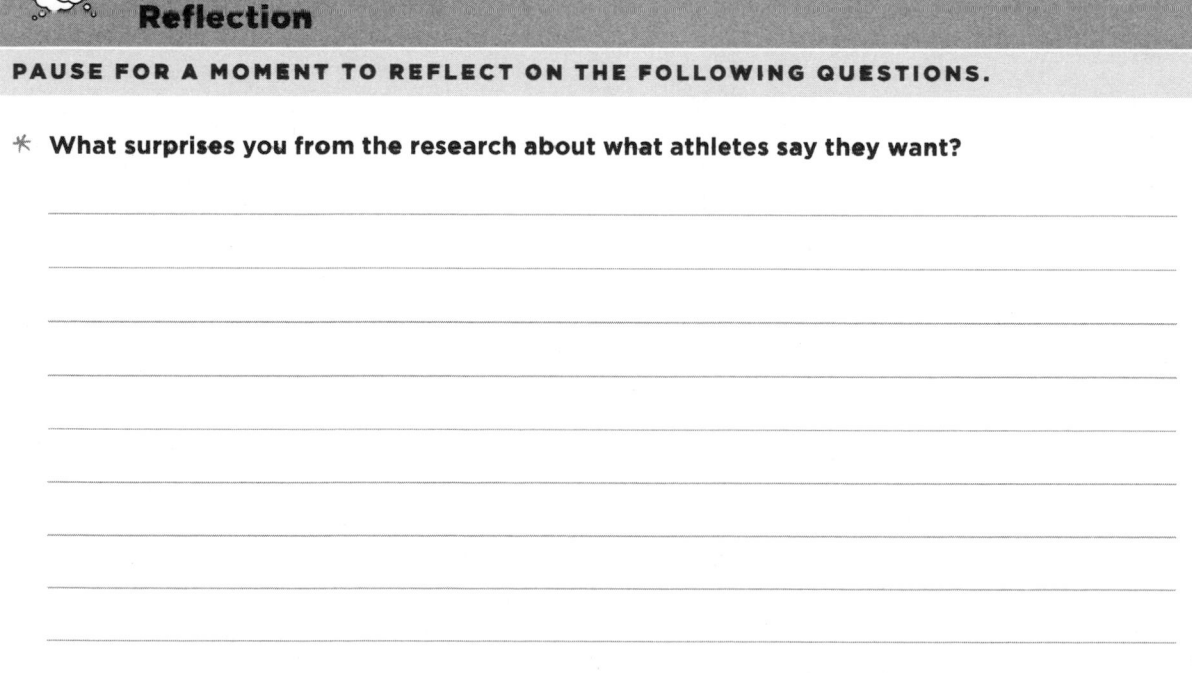

Reflection

PAUSE FOR A MOMENT TO REFLECT ON THE FOLLOWING QUESTIONS.

✳ **What surprises you from the research about what athletes say they want?**

_____

_____

_____

_____

_____

_____

_____

_____

_____

✳ **Where have you seen intrinsic versus extrinsic motivation at work with other coaches and players?**

_____

_____

_____

_____

_____

_____

_____

_____

_____

✳ **Is motivation something you actively think about with your athletes? Why or why not?**

_____

_____

_____

_____

_____

_____

_____

_____

Implications for Coaches

What do these findings mean for coaches? And how do coaches' shifts in practice affect players? See what happens when we apply the psychological understanding of child development to sports.

IMPLEMENTING THE PRACTICE CYCLE

Piaget (1951) argued children learn best about their world by interacting with it. A coach might respond to this by telling players about the expectations for an upcoming drill. This is a start, but this coach can take it even further by stating the expectations while modeling them before the practice drill. More players *doing* the drills is ultimately best. Figure 2.2 demonstrates how to implement this as a practice cycle.

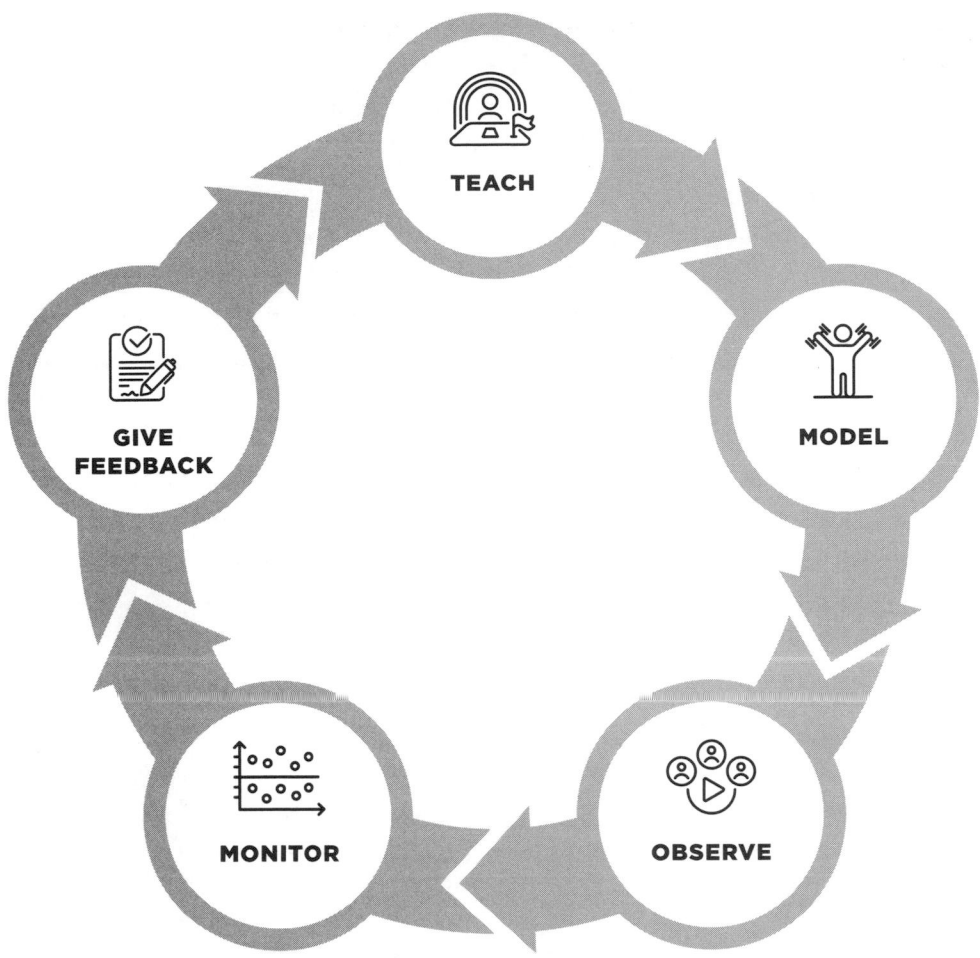

Figure 2.2: Practice cycle.

The following is a look at each of these elements in more detail.

- **Teach:** Teach the skill. Clearly consider the progressions the drill will exemplify.

- **Model:** Explicitly state your expectations and the form you expect to see. It is particularly helpful if a coach can do this, as players inherently garner increased respect for a coach who can do what that coach is asking of the players. If this isn't possible, then use a video or an actual player as a model to demonstrate.

- **Observe:** Watch each player carefully. What is the player doing well? What specifically is inhibiting the player's progress? Consider video recording each player's performance for a coach and player reflection later.

- **Monitor:** Attend to the time, intensity, and flow you expect. Be aware of which players need positive reinforcement for executing the skill at a high level, versus those who need more refinement or those who might need to be stopped to correct a major error. The developmental sports scales introduced in chapter 3 (page 58) are a great tool to use during this step.

- **Give feedback:** After monitoring each player, make mental or physical notes. Then, consider how best to share positive or corrective feedback. Is it better to stop the drill to share or can you share throughout the drill? How egregious is the error you noted? If the error will foster poor habits, you may need to pull the player aside to reteach and remodel the expectation immediately. Other times you may finish or pause the drill, share what you are noticing, and resume the drill expecting the necessary corrections.

Without dedicating themselves to a practice cycle like the one in figure 2.2 (page 37), coaches may lapse into talking, lecturing, or ranting, but doing so isn't effective for holding players' attention and enacting the changes coaches wish to see in player performance. The practice cycle helps players solidify their understanding of the key knowledge, skills, and intangibles they need to thrive. Focus on having your players spend more time *doing*. Increase the number of active touches and game-like experiences by increasing the number of lines in a drill with fewer waiting or inactive players. For example, instead of two lines of ten players in each, create four lines with five players in each. This doubles the number of active practices for each player. Maybe even better would be six lines of three or four players in each. This seemingly small adjustment increases active experiences, keeps players more involved and engaged, and may even reduce the need for overall (often unrelated) conditioning, since players are more often moving and participating. To use the practice cycle with your team, access the reproducible "Implementing the Practice Cycle" at the end of this chapter (page 49).

Reflection

PAUSE FOR A MOMENT TO REFLECT ON THE FOLLOWING QUESTIONS.

✴ **What do you think about this practice cycle?**

_____

_____

_____

_____

_____

✴ **If someone were to walk into your practice, which of these aspects would they see most? Least?**

_____

_____

_____

_____

_____

✳ **What changes will you make to implement this practice cycle?**

_____

_____

_____

_____

_____

_____

CONSIDERING PLAYERS' NEEDS

What does Maslow's (1943, 1954, 1969, 1979) hierarchy of needs mean for how coaches understand and interact with players? Athletes' position on the hierarchy of needs determines their capacity to show up to each practice and team event.

As you might imagine, if players aren't properly nourished or hydrated, their performance will be affected in practice or games. An awareness of your players' home life and challenges may give insight into why they aren't performing as you expect. If they are consumed with where they will sleep or where to find food, practice likely can't be their top priority.

If players are being subjected to physical or emotional harm—through bullying, harassment, or abuse—they will likely be consumed with ensuring their safety needs are met and may have little capacity to focus on practice.

If players are worried more about which group they are practicing with or which team they perceive they are on at the time, their need to belong may inadvertently consume them. Coaches can mix things up, assigning players to work with different peers during practice and paying attention to how players respond. Pay attention to players' sense of belonging. Be wary of having captains select players for scrimmages and the like. Remember, having a sense of belonging is a critical human need for all your players.

Players' esteem is partly what they believe about themselves, and partly what they perceive others believe about them. How other people perceive a person's sense of worth impacts that person to some extent. Consider the relational dynamics of your team. How do players treat one another on the field, in the locker room, on the bus, at practice, and during a game? These dynamics have a strong influence on players' esteem. What kinds of expectations do you set for relational dynamics on the team? What you model and tolerate are what you can expect to see from players. Make sure your players' needs for respect, recognition, and their peers' esteem influences the environment you cultivate in your program.

Ultimately, coaches want players to reach the top of Maslow's (1943, 1954, 1969, 1979) hierarchy; coaches want players to achieve self-actualization and strive to support others in pursuing their full potential. Imagine a team full of self-actualized players! What would your program look like if the physiological, safety, belonging, and esteem needs of players each were met and they were empowered to pursue their full potential? This is where you are trying to get your players. You want them to develop themselves to the best they each can be. How you help them meet those lower needs makes a huge impact not only on each player but also on the team as a whole.

Reflection

PAUSE FOR A MOMENT TO REFLECT ON THE FOLLOWING QUESTIONS.

✳ **Do you know your players well enough to understand their needs? If not, what habits can you foster to get to know them and better recognize their needs?**

_____

_____

_____

_____

_____

_____

_____

✳ **How might you consider Maslow's (1943, 1954, 1969, 1979) hierarchy as you frame practices? Competitions?**

_____

_____

_____

_____

_____

_____

✳ **At which level is each of your players currently? How might you support each player to move up?**

_____

_____

_____

_____

_____

_____

_____

Foster Positive Player-Coach Relationships

MOTIVATING PLAYERS FROM THE INSIDE OUT

Deci and Ryan's (2008) research suggested coaches must consider the motivational aspect of player psychology if they want athletes to reach their potential. Players may respond to external pressures with extrinsic behaviors, but it's unsustainable over the long term. Don't settle for extrinsic forms of motivation. Cultivate habits and routines that nurture players' intrinsic motivation, and your team will thrive for the right reasons. Keep it interesting. Keep the goals attainable and foster player autonomy by infusing your expectations clearly throughout your program. If you want your players to share your vision, you must understand what they care about and help them understand how your interests align. Chapter 3 (page 51) includes strategies for increasing intrinsic motivation using developmental sports scales. Using these scales for clarification, player reflection, and quality feedback from your coaching team moves players from extrinsic to intrinsic motivations.

This shift is especially important given that research shows a downward trend in youth physical activity (Cavill, Kahlmeier, & Racioppi, 2006; Ogden, Carroll, & Flegal, 2008; World Health Organization & Food and Agriculture Organization of the United Nations, 2003). Youth's movement habits—and, consequently, their bodies—are changing. Virtually one-third of youth are overweight, and half of those are obese. They spend more and more time in front of screens obtaining almost specific and immediate feedback in virtual environments, exacerbating their disinterest in being active in outdoor sports. Interestingly, fewer than 1 percent of sports sociology papers consulted children in their studies of youth sports (Aspen Institute, n.d.e). The Aspen Institute (n.d.e) argues studies should remedy this oversight as a way of understanding what youth want:

It's Rule No. 1 in business: know your customer. Video games (and technology industry more broadly) often get blamed for our kids' sedentary habits, yet they provide much of what children want out of a sport experience, including: lots of action, freedom to experiment, competition without exclusion, social connection with friends as co-players, customization, and a measure of control over the activity—plus, no parents critiquing their every move. Simply the child is at the center of the video game experience, all made possible by research and feedback loops that seek input from its young customers. (p. 12)

What if youth sports coaches used this idea with athletes? How might they better engage and coach players? Often, coaches lean on personal past experiences to plan for student athletes, and while their professional insight is valuable, it doesn't leave space for team members to participate in creating their learning. What if, instead, coaches asked players what matters to them? When coaches listen to students and implement their ideas whenever possible, they invest in intrinsic motivation. Pause for a moment and imagine what this might look like with your players. How might it inform your choices, routines, and habits? How might it shape your relationship with players individually and the team as a whole? Would your players be surprised to be included in influencing the athletic program? Would the kinds of answers you receive surprise you and your coaching staff?

Often, as a coach, you are in a unique position to see your players in many stages and phases. You see them at practices and notice their perseverance through new and difficult tasks. You observe them in game situations where pressure accentuates and stresses their performances. You likely see them socially with other players and friends on the road trips to and from competitions. Most likely, you see them at their best and worst moments. Your keen ability to understand, assist, and support makes for great player-coach relationships. Having a basic understanding of the psychological elements of players and their performances will help you better understand how to help them become their best.

Reflection

PAUSE FOR A MOMENT TO REFLECT ON THE FOLLOWING QUESTIONS.

* **What came to mind as you read about extrinsic versus intrinsic motivation?**

_____

_____

_____

_____

_____

_____

* **How can you work to foster more intrinsic motivation with your athletes?**

_____

_____

_____

_____

_____

_____

* **What changes will you make as a result of this information?**

_____

_____

_____

_____

_____

_____

Successful Player-Coach Relationships

We identified the building of relationships with your players as an essential coaching characteristic in chapter 1 (page 13). In this section, we draw from our wealth of experiences to share additional ways to foster successful player-coach relationships.

Players each thrive with a positive coaching relationship. While some players may like the coach to push them directly and regularly, others may need more positive reinforcement. The key is not assuming what each player needs, but finding out. Ask your players: "What do you need from me to improve your practice?" If they are unable to detail what they need, provide players with examples such as: "Are you better when I verbally express what you need to do? Do you need to see visuals before practice to help you know what we are doing and why? Do videos help you fine-tune your practice?" Whatever you do, *don't assume*. Showing you care enough to ask helps you build those important relationships with your athletes.

As a coach, students *will* remember you. *How* they remember you is up to you. We remember amazing coaches! They inspired us. They pushed us to levels we didn't even know we could attain. They were honest and fair. They cared. They even made us want to become just like them! The power of a great coach is immeasurable and life impacting. In "The Crucial Coaching Relationship," developmental psychologist Peter C. Scales (2016) wrote about *developmental relationships*—those close connections coaches initiate that empower players to develop character, gain confidence in their identity, and take autonomy over their lives:

> When students have developmental relationships, they're more engaged in school, get better grades, have better mental health, are more socially competent, engage less in high-risk behavior, and have more grit, mental toughness, and perseverance than students lacking in developmental relationships (Pekel, Roehlkepartain, Syvertsen, & Scales, 2015).

How do you want players to remember you? Competent? Relational? Funny? Helpful? Think about this. Then, purposefully work on your player-coach relationships to foster what you want. Consider the following aspects of nurturing relationships with athletes.

Your behavior sets the expectations for how your players will behave. If you want your players to act with integrity, you must model integrity. Say what you expect and do what you say. Your players notice. Their parents notice. Your reputation will outlive your time as a coach. How you shape it is up to you!

Athletes listen to you. *What* you say and *how* you say it has a significant impact on them. This is a key way to meet those human needs for belonging and esteem. Don't berate players. Don't insult them. Make sure your words support athletes' intrinsic motivation. In the long term, this is how coaches sustain positive relationships with players. Your players may not remember the score or their teammates all that much, but they will remember your relationship with them.

Players pay attention to how you respond to challenges, especially the challenge of losing the game, the match, the tournament, the championship. How you prepare, learn, and bounce back is important. Nothing you do goes unnoticed. Be a good loser. Be gracious to your other coaches. Don't blame. Don't shame. Be respectful to the opposing coaches. Thank the referees or umpires. Acknowledge when you got outplayed, outscored, and yes, maybe even outcoached. It doesn't mean you can't be frustrated or even admit that you're angry. How you share those emotions is what your players (and their parents) will remember.

Seeking to understand the role of the player-coach relationship on athlete success, the University of Florida Sport Policy and Research Collaborative discovered:

> Critical to the development of elite athletes was quality coaching at a young age. . . . The survey found that U.S. Olympians from 1984–98 indicated that excellent coaches ranked as the third-most important factor that contributed to their success as an Olympic athlete. Excellent coaches ranked just below *dedication and persistence* and *support of family and friends* . . . 673 elite athletes (including 51 Olympians) in Australia further emphasized how important coaching is even during the sampling phases of sport participation . . . the critical influence of a coach as a young athlete was their *"ability to motivate and encourage."* (as cited in Aspen Institute, n.d.f, p. 3)

Be the kind of coach you would want for your own children or loved ones. What you do every single day matters; athletes will remember you. Make them good memories!

Reflection

PAUSE FOR A MOMENT TO REFLECT ON THE FOLLOWING QUESTIONS.

* **What is your current relationship with your athletes? How do you know? What are the strengths and weaknesses of these relationships?**

_____

_____

_____

_____

_____

_____

_____

_____

_____

_____

✳ **What steps will you take to foster a more positive relationship with each of your players?**

_____

_____

_____

_____

_____

✳ **What will you do to be more aware of each player's needs and level of motivation?**

_____

_____

_____

_____

_____

Activities for Team Building

Building a strong team isn't just about each player becoming proficient in the sport's knowledge and skills; it's also about the bond all players share as a team. Nurturing and solidifying that bond is part of the coach's job. Thoughtfully considering how your players feel about one another will affect their willingness to support, challenge, and help their peers. Even athletes playing individual sports often have connections to other competitors. Athletes may run cross country alone, but they are still part of the cross country team; wrestlers compete individually, but they are part of the wrestling team; and gymnasts vie independently on the parallel bars as part of the gymnastics team. Therefore, it is important to infuse team-building protocols throughout practices for all sports. It is especially important at the beginning of the season, when players are just getting to know one another and their roles as teammates.

Team-building protocols are also essential when problems arise among players. There will be jealousy, frustrations, and even confrontations among your athletes. Acknowledge and address these—the dynamics of your team depends on it, and doing so offers you a unique opportunity to mentor youth athletes on how to resolve conflict with maturity. Unresolved conflict festers and often seems to erupt at the time you need athletes to support and help one another most—like at major tournaments, end-of-season games, and championship matches. Build a strong team—the kind where players care about each other beyond the field, court, pitch, or pool. Build positive relationships with your players. Be a coach your players will call when they want to share a joyous accomplishment or struggle they're experiencing. Be there for them. Be the person players can come to when something big is going on in their lives. Consider the following team-building activities, which you can add into practice time.

NOTE CARD NOTICE

Make note cards with the name of one player at the top of each. Ask your players to take a note card at the beginning of practice; their job is to find one positive thing the person (noted at the top of the card) did during practice that day. Extend it throughout the week if you like. It's fun to have the observing players not reveal who they are watching. After the designated time frame, players write one or two positive attributes or contributions they noticed and then share their card with the player they observed. Figure 2.3 shows an example of how a player might complete this activity.

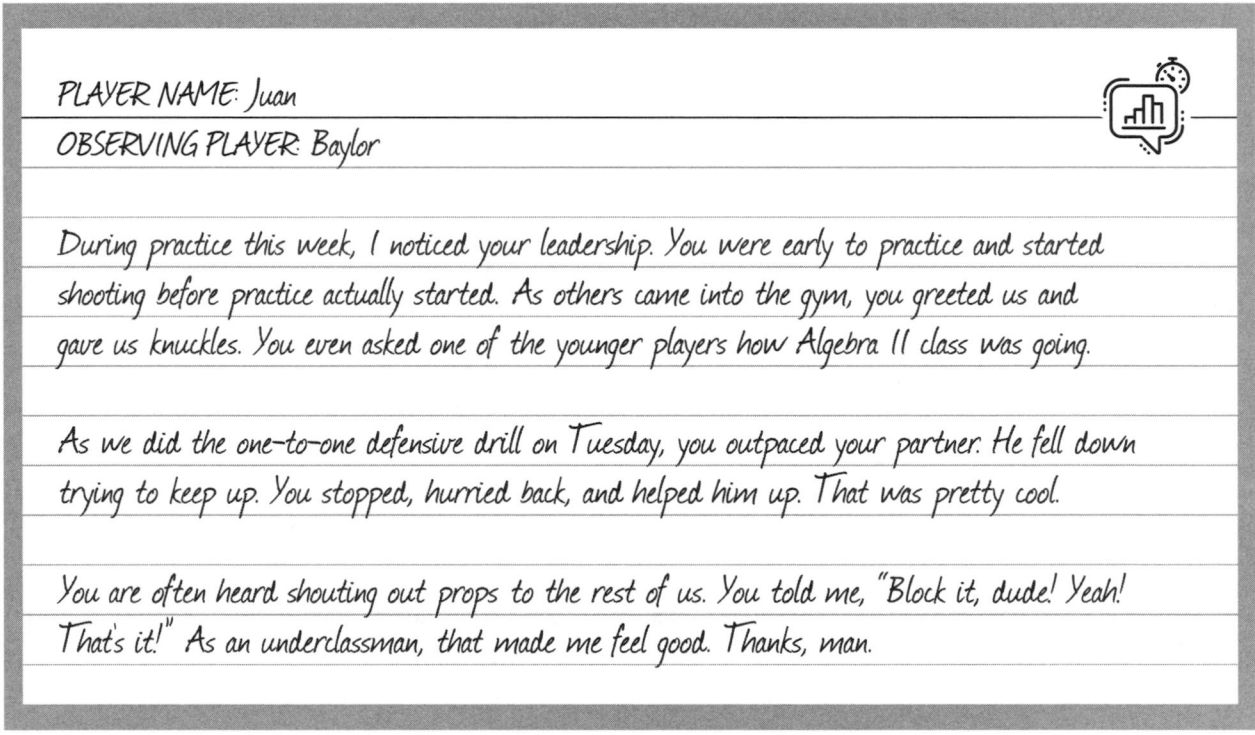

PLAYER NAME: Juan
OBSERVING PLAYER: Baylor

During practice this week, I noticed your leadership. You were early to practice and started shooting before practice actually started. As others came into the gym, you greeted us and gave us knuckles. You even asked one of the younger players how Algebra II class was going.

As we did the one-to-one defensive drill on Tuesday, you outpaced your partner. He fell down trying to keep up. You stopped, hurried back, and helped him up. That was pretty cool.

You are often heard shouting out props to the rest of us. You told me, "Block it, dude! Yeah! That's it!" As an underclassman, that made me feel good. Thanks, man.

Figure 2.3: Sample student note card.

You may invite a couple of players to share their note cards with the group, but this sharing should be optional. Sometimes when players hear some of the examples, it helps them improve their specificity for later exchanges. Vary this process as you desire, but get your team to notice positive things about others. What you pay attention to you get more of.

RELIC BAG

This one comes from Tammy's book *Crafting Your Message: Tips and Tricks for Educators to Deliver Perfect Presentations* in which she shares presentation strategies for team building (Heflebower, 2020). For this activity, ask players to bring a valuable item (or picture of that item) to a designated practice. Divide your team into smaller groups and have players each describe their relic for about two minutes. For instance, one player might bring a necklace with his grandpa's ashes in it; another might share a note a coach wrote to her when she was younger; yet another might be his favorite chocolate bar. The point is, teammates learn something about others they didn't know before. Understanding builds teams. Think of it like this: *if I don't know who you are, I won't care what you think or contribute to our team.*

LIFE BOXES

To try another of Tammy's team building activities, bring a sheet of paper and a pen or pencil for each player (Heflebower, 2020). Ask players to fold the paper in half, and in half again so there are four squares. Have players write titles for each square. They could be (1) childhood experience, (2) a favorite memory, (3) someone you admire, (4) a struggle you overcame. You can easily modify these titles to fit your team. Next, in each of the life boxes, have players draw a simple picture that represents something related to the title. Have them share these drawings with the team.

Although you might be saying to yourself, "When will I find time to do this soft stuff?" we argue it will be time well spent. If your players don't care about one another, they won't battle for one another on the field, pitch, court, or mat.

The options are endless. Use the ideas featured here to help you get started. For more team-building activities, see "Twenty Team Building Exercises for Youth Sports" (Vossekuil, n.d.; https://signupgenius .com/sports/team-building-sports.cfm). As you continue to work to build your team, you can also design your own activities. Let your players' unique personalities and relationships lead the way. What kinds of activities might you design that feel authentic to both you and them? Remember, you are building more than a win-loss record. You are building relationships. You are building a team.

 Reflection

PAUSE FOR A MOMENT TO REFLECT ON THE FOLLOWING QUESTIONS.

✳ **What is an influential team-building activity you've experienced that you could use with your players?**

_____

_____

_____

_____

_____

_____

_____

* **Do you practice team building with your coaching staff?**

_____

_____

_____

_____

_____

_____

* **Where can you look for ideas and inspiration for further team building?**

_____

_____

_____

_____

_____

_____

_____

_____

Summary

In this chapter, we considered child-development models and how they inform the coach's relationship to athletes' cognitive development, the hierarchy of needs, and the motivational types. We explored the implications for coaches, such as constructing a practice cycle, considering player' needs, and boosting intrinsic motivation. We also included considerations for fostering player-coach relationships and activities for team building.

We pointed out in this chapter the secret to the body is through the brain. When coaches learn to recognize and respect players' stages of development (understanding the advantages and challenges of the stage each player is in), they can work with, rather than against, a player's cognitive development. For the scope of this book, we turned to the work of Piaget (1951), Maslow (1943, 1954, 1969, 1979), and Deci and Ryan (1985, 2008) to extrapolate the implications of a coach's work with players.

It is essential that coaches understand their athletes' psychological development. This allows coaches to set realistic expectations, address players' most basic human needs, and consider how to foster intrinsic motivation. With the foundation of positive player-coach relationships and a strong team bond, coaches can focus their efforts on monitoring and assessing players proficiency in key knowledge, skills, and intangibles of their sport.

Implementing the Practice Cycle

Use the following chart to review each step of the practice cycle and plan for implementation. In the third column, take notes about how you will implement each step with players.

Step	Description	Notes for Implementation
Teach	Teach the skill, clearly explaining the progressions players should exemplify in the drill.	
Model	Explicitly state your expectations and demonstrate the form, using a video or a model as needed.	
Observe	Carefully watch each player, noticing what each player is doing well and what elements are inhibiting progress.	
Monitor	Monitor each player's performance during practices and competitions, assessing each player's mastery of the form you expect.	
Give feedback	Give players verbal and written feedback that reinforces their growth and communicates areas for improvement. Feedback may take various forms at various times, including developmental sports scales (see chapter 4, page 80).	

CHAPTER 3

Determine What You Will Teach and Assess

As a player, did you ever wonder why you weren't getting more playing time or playing a position you wanted? Were you sometimes afraid to ask, fearing it might limit your role even more? As a coach, have you observed parents becoming too involved in questioning your decisions or criticizing your strategic planning? In some cases, it may have gone further, involving your athletic or program director. Such issues are time-consuming and may even cause more than a few sleepless nights. What if you could mitigate these issues by providing the clarity to your players (and indirectly to their parents) in thorough and thoughtful ways *prior* to an incident? What if you could substantiate your decisions easily through more objective means?

In this chapter, we establish expectations for proficiency-based coaching. This concept involves a series of processes and products coaches use to select the most important knowledge and skills, clearly articulate them, and use them as tools for athlete self-reflection. They also empower coaching staff to evaluate athletes' progress and offer quality feedback for improvement. We begin by introducing a process coaches can use to identify priority knowledge and skills athletes need to thrive in their sport. Then we introduce the *developmental sports scale*, a tool for communicating those expectations to athletes and assessing their proficiency. Learning a sport is a bit messy, but it shouldn't be a mystery. By clarifying the expectations for yourself, other staff members, and players, you prepare all for increased ownership and success.

Proficiency-Based Coaching

For athletes to clearly learn the knowledge and skills for success in a sport, the coach must first determine what is most critical to know, by when, and how players attain and demonstrate proficiency. Players are continuously completing mini-performance tasks in practices and competitions. As simple as it may appear, assessing player learning presents the coach with some complicated questions—often without readily apparent answers. For example, consider the following questions.

- What content and skills are important for the sport?
- How often should the coach teach content and skills?
- When should the coach evaluate players?
- How might players use self-assessment and feedback for setting goals?
- How will the coach share and use players' skills to determine playing time?

Although it's natural for the answers to such questions to evolve over time, coaches should be able to answer the final question in the list—an issue we will discuss in more detail throughout this chapter. Coaches use the information they obtain from performances to inform many aspects of the sport, including providing feedback to players and reporting player progress. Yet, all this should be built on a solid foundation: the knowledge, skills, and intangibles the coach identifies as being essential for player success.

In *Planning and Teaching in the Standards-Based Classroom*, coauthors Jeff Flygare, Jan K. Hoegh, and Tammy Heflebower (2022) call classroom teachers to shift to standards-based learning, aligning instruction with essential standards to ensure *all* students learn. In short, it's about "making sure that selected instructional strategies help students develop the specific knowledge and skills required by the standards" (Flygare et al., 2022, p. 2). They explain:

> To make the standards more functional for instruction, educators can craft *learning progressions* that define basic, target, and advanced levels of a standard or a closely related group of standards. . . . When creating a proficiency scale, an educator uses the standard as a starting point to write learning targets for each level of the scale. These learning targets represent three levels: content that is simpler and therefore a prerequisite to reaching proficiency on the standard, content at the level of the standard, and more complex content that is beyond the standard. These learning progressions scaffold student learning and guide teachers' unit and lesson planning. In fact, proficiency scales become a central tool of instruction, assessment, and feedback, with lessons, test questions, and scores all based on the scale. Because the scales are an augmentation of the standards themselves, lessons, test items, and scores related to scales are also standards based. (Flygare et al., 2022, p. 4)

Determine What You Will Teach and Assess

The same concept applies for coaches supporting players to reach proficiency in the necessary knowledge and skills of their sport. The format Flygare and colleagues (2022) recommended was the *proficiency scale* education researcher Robert J. Marzano (2006, 2009) used (see figure 3.1). For our purposes in this book, we refer to these scales as *developmental sports scales*, customizing the levels to suit an athletic context.

4.0		In addition to score 3.0 performance, the student demonstrates in-depth inferences and applications that go beyond what was taught
	3.5	In addition to score 3.0 performance, partial success at score 4.0 content
3.0		Target goal
	2.5	No major errors or omissions regarding score 2.0 content and partial success at score 3.0 content
2.0		Simpler goal
	1.5	Partial success at score 2.0 content and major errors or omissions regarding score 3.0 content
1.0		With help, partial success at score 2.0 content and score 3.0 content
	0.5	With help, partial success at score 2.0 content but not at score 3.0 content
0.0		Even with help, no success

Source: Adapted from Marzano, 2006, 2010, 2017.

Figure 3.1: Generic form of a proficiency scale.

*Visit **MarzanoResources.com/reproducibles** for a blank reproducible version of this figure.*

Reflection

PAUSE FOR A MOMENT TO REFLECT ON THE FOLLOWING QUESTIONS.

* **What questions most often come up for you about player proficiency?**

_____

_____

_____

_____

_____

_____

_____

✳ **Have you identified the essential knowledge, skills, and intangibles your athletes need to succeed?**

_____

_____

_____

_____

_____

_____

✳ **Are there any questions included in this section you haven't considered?**

_____

_____

_____

_____

_____

_____

Determine What You Will Teach and Assess

Priority Knowledge, Skills, and Intangibles

Just as classroom teachers use the standards-based approach to monitor student proficiency of essential skills, coaches can identify priority knowledge and skills players should master for their particular sport. Identifying priority skills allows coaches to go deep into the essentials. Educational researchers Robert J. Marzano, David C. Yanoski, and Diane E. Paynter (2016) determined teachers simply do not have sufficient class time during the K–12 years to bring all students to proficiency on each state standard. If teachers don't narrow the curriculum to a set of essential priorities, teachers find themselves moving rapidly through an enormous amount of content, often not having the time to ensure student proficiency on the required standards. This is true for coaches too—they must determine what knowledge, skills, and intangibles are most essential for athletes to master.

Coaches should also include intangibles alongside the priority knowledge and skills they expect players to master in their sport. *Intangibles* refer to behavioral skills, like effort, attitude, work ethic, timeliness, and so on, essential for athletes to thrive. Head coach of the Ohio Force of Major League Football Bill Conley (2008) wrote about this in an article for ESPN:

> College coaches continually look for the ideal athlete for each position on the football team. The vitally important physical elements—height, weight, speed, quickness, leaping ability, change of direction, strength and technical skills—are among the characteristics evaluated by coaches before making that highly sought-after scholarship offer.

It's amazing, however, how often it's true that an abundance of physical talent doesn't translate to success on the gridiron. There are other factors—the proverbial intangibles—which can indeed be the difference between mediocre and being exceptional. . . . These intangibles are sometimes difficult to measure, but any college coach will tell you they are worth their weight in gold.

These intangibles are key for athletes to be great in their sport. It does not take physical talent to give all your effort during drills and games. This is often an intrinsic quality athletes demand of themselves. In many situations, these intangibles are the difference between a starter and nonstarter, a position player and backup, an athletic leader and follower. Although it's sometimes difficult to clarify these qualities, it is possible. Throughout this book, we identify intangibles important in most sports and provide the clarity to teach and measure them.

Consider the following five key criteria for identifying essential knowledge, skills, and intangibles. The first three are based on educational consultant and author Larry Ainsworth's (2003) recommendations for K–12 teachers, while the last two come from the work of coauthors Tammy Heflebower, Jan K. Hoegh, and Philip B. Warrick (2014).

1. **Endurance:** Knowledge and skills players should retain over a long period of time, rather than just for a particular level or season

2. **Leverage:** Knowledge and skills important in a different sport outside the one in which the player is currently engaged

3. **Readiness:** Knowledge and skills essential for the next or additional levels of playing the sport

4. **Performance evaluation:** Knowledge and skills universally important in the players' future

5. **Coaching judgment:** Coaches with experience in the content or sport identify essential knowledge and skills

Using these five criteria in a matrix like the one in figure 3.2 (page 56), coaches can identify a set of priority skills that represent the essential content and level for a specific sport. Coaches then address all priority skills during practice or games; these skills become the focus of performance evaluations.

To get started, think about a few key roles on your team. For example, in football it might be the quarterback (on offense), a linebacker (on defense), and a kicker (on special teams). Although all positions are important and have their unique considerations, begin with the pivotal roles and expand from there. When beginning this process, start independently—even if you have a coaching team. This provides you time to become comfortable with the process. In the matrix, list all knowledge, skills, and intangibles you deem essential for an athlete to master the sport in the first column (see figure 3.2, page 56). Then consider which of the five criteria apply for that item. For instance, think about competent athletes in your sport. Ask yourself, "What do they know almost instinctively? What do they do? How do they move or position themselves?" Now, name such knowledge and skills. For example, a great volleyball player effectively serves to various areas of the court on request. So, serving is a key skill. As we take this further into the developmental sports scales later, we will break down each of those essential skills into various components (in this case, footwork, ball toss, ball contact, and arm follow-through).

	ENDURANCE (Beyond the season)	LEVERAGE (Useful in other sports)	READINESS (Important for the next level of play)	PERFORMANCE EVALUATION (Key element for performing effectively in this sport)	(MY) COACHING JUDGMENT (Important to me and my approach to the sport)
Serving: Effectively merge footwork with shoulder position and ball contact to start play	X	X	X	X	X
Passing: Able to move to the ball, and to use arm platform and shoulder angles correctly	X		X	X	X
Attacking: Approach ball with effective planting, jumping, shoulder position, and hand contact	X		X	X	X
Blocking: Demonstrate efficient footwork, planting, jumping, arm, and hand positioning, with looking at hitter to ball, then to hand	X		X	X	X
Court sense: Know where each player is located during different plays	X		X	X	X
Setting: Demonstrate proper hand and finger positioning for soft ball contact, release, arm power, and direction	X		X	X	
Knowledge of offenses and defenses	X		X	X	X
Communication	X	X			X
Effort	X	X	X	X	X
Attitude	X	X	X	X	X

Source: Adapted from Heflebower et al., 2014.

Figure 3.2: Matrix for identifying key knowledge, skills, and intangibles.
*Visit **MarzanoResources.com/reproducibles** for a blank reproducible version of this figure.*

Figure 3.2 shows an example of how a coach might complete this task for volleyball. (To complete this task for positions on your team, visit ***MarzanoResources.com/reproducibles*** to download a reproducible version of this figure.) Once you feel you've mastered this process, share it with your coaching team and provide the resources to repeat the process with their athletes.

In figure 3.2 you can see how some items have more *Xs* and constitute a greater emphasis than others. Items that fulfill all five criteria are your priority knowledge and skills. For example, serving meets all criteria. This skill has endurance because players will use it beyond this season for many years and seasons to come; it has leverage because it infuses the ability to throw overhand, a skill noted in other sports like softball, soccer, baseball, and football. Serving has readiness because it is foundational for more complex serving skills, like placing serves in specific court locations and infusing various spins or floaters in higher levels of play. Coaches also regularly monitor and evaluate serving, and it is essential to the start of play in volleyball. Missing a serve immediately provides a point to the opponent. High-level players and coaches also deem serving important. While the skill of communication may have some measure of endurance and leverage, it doesn't tick the Readiness and Evaluation boxes. It's tempting to see all skills as important; yet, given that resources are limited, coaches must determine where to direct their time and attention. It is also important to note the three intangible skills of (1) communication, (2) effort, and (3) attitude are part of this process. Both effort and attitude will be essential for any sport and meet all the criteria, whereas communication may be slightly less important, depending on the position and sport.

After each coaching team member independently completes the matrix of criteria for a specific sport and level, meet and compare results. If you don't have other coaches, reference the developmental sports scales in the appendixes (beginning on page 115). Coaches and players with a wealth of experience in the sport designed these scales. Whether you're working with a team or drawing inspiration from the sample scales, compile your results into a comprehensive list of five to eight priority knowledge, skills, and intangibles per each criterion for your sport and grade level. Use fewer for younger players (up to age ten or eleven) and more for those in elite programs and at the college level.

Once you identify a set of priority skills, you are well on your way to identifying what is important enough to teach, monitor, and evaluate. Your priority skills will constitute the bulk of practice, and they will generally identify the essential content you use to assess players. Priority skills will also identify the consistent topics for all coaches on that team's coaching staff. Additionally, coaches use these assessments to provide feedback to players, identify starting and secondary teams, and allocate playing time. Players will also use them for self-assessment purposes.

It can sometimes be true that a single priority skill may require more than a single developmental sports scale. For example, a complex skill like serving in volleyball requires quite a few important components, such as footwork, toss, shoulder alignment, ball contact, and ball placement. Depending on the level you are coaching, you may have a scale for the footwork and one for the ball contact and placement. It is also possible to represent multiple skills on a single developmental sports scale. This is most often the case. By unpacking the skills and understanding the progression leading to player proficiency on those skills, coaches can create practice opportunities to identify player needs and progress at each point of the skill progression. Using developmental sports scales helps eliminate a good deal of the work for coaches in understanding the details about each priority skill.

Reflection

PAUSE FOR A MOMENT TO REFLECT ON THE FOLLOWING QUESTIONS.

✳ **What knowledge, skills, and intangibles come to mind as being essential to your sport?**

_____

_____

_____

_____

_____

✳ **How many essential skills would be reasonable for your sport? Which intangibles should you include?**

_____

_____

_____

_____

_____

✳ **How would your coaching staff and team benefit from working with the matrix in this section?**

_____

_____

_____

_____

_____

_____

Determine What You Will Teach and Assess

Developmental Sports Scales

Just as teachers scaffold learning for K–12 students, effective coaches scaffold knowledge, skills, and intangibles for players, building more complex knowledge on the foundation of simpler knowledge and skills about the sport. The developmental sports scale is a great tool for this approach, outlining the scaffolded knowledge and skills and clarifying the player's path toward proficiency. Even veteran coaches rely on developmental sports scales to clarify what they are doing during a practice or competition. These scales clarify what is important and what each priority skill looks like as players develop.

Once coaches identify the priority skills, they will need a way of measuring player progress toward proficiency. This is one of the purposes of the developmental sports scale (Heflebower, 2005; Heflebower, Hoegh, & Warrick, 2014; Heflebower, Hoegh, Warrick, & Flygare, 2019; Marzano, 2006, 2010, 2017). It is useful to think in terms of a developmental sports scale for each priority skill you identified through the process.

A *priority skill* informs the player's progression in the developmental sports scale. In the scale, there are any number of *components* that represent specific learning goals players must achieve during the journey to proficiency. These components will usually fall at score 1.0 on the developmental sports scale. Components can also represent pieces of the overall skill and thus reside at score 2.0 on the scale. In this case, coaches would instruct each component, identifying a player as proficient on the skill when the player has mastered all those pieces. Further, most developmental sports scales identify components at score 3.0, which represents learning that exceeds the typical criteria for the developmental sports scale and may be seen only in elite athletes.

Here is an example and break down what this process might look like. In the instance of serving as a volleyball skill, the process could unfold as follows.

- Drill down into the more specific components of footwork, ball toss, ball contact, and arm follow-through.

- List each component at the proficient level (2.0) on the developmental sports scale.

- Take one of the components and think about what describes that specific skill at the proficient level. This usually requires adding a verb phrase like *balancing the weight on your feet* or *transferring the weight from your back foot to your front foot while contacting the ball*.

- To design the level 1.0 content, think about what you see in players who are not quite reaching proficiency. What does that look like? Perhaps the player transfers weight from the back foot to the front foot before contacting the ball.

- Construct statements that communicate this lack of proficiency in positive terms, and whenever possible, focus on describing what players achieve rather than fail to achieve. If this isn't possible (and at times, it's not), use positive language to motivate players to reach proficiency. You can do this by thinking about what you *do* see, rather than what you *don't* see. What are common errors the players make? If possible, reflect on these common errors using nonjudgmental language such as *inefficiently* rather than *poorly*.

- Next, consider what an advanced player may do. In the example of volleyball, this would be a *jump serve*. The player transfers the weight of the feet (as in an approach) to attack the ball. The player starts with one foot behind the other, then takes a *gather step* (right then left) that begins the jump.

Each coach may approach this process slightly differently, but the focus is on articulating the skills into the basic components. Think about how you would show a beginner an essential skill in your sport. You would do each part deliberately to emphasize each component, then slowly put them together faster and faster until they are fluid and habitual. By first thinking about what you want at proficiency, you can better divide the skill into the beginning level, and then extrapolate the advanced level afterward.

Given that developmental sports scales identify performance at different levels relative to criteria and identify practice components at each level of the scale, it's a useful tool for coaches to scaffold learning for players as they journey to proficiency in the essential knowledge, skills, and intangibles of their sport.

Reflection

PAUSE FOR A MOMENT TO REFLECT ON THE FOLLOWING QUESTIONS.

* **How do you currently identify the skills for your athletes to focus on during practice?**

_____

_____

_____

_____

_____

_____

_____

* **How do you measure players' progress in reaching proficiency with these skills?**

_____

_____

_____

_____

_____

_____

_____

_____

* **How does the developmental sports scale template help or differ from your current method?**

_____

_____

_____

_____

_____

_____

_____

_____

Determine What You Will Teach and Assess

CUSTOMIZED DEVELOPMENTAL SPORTS SCALES

Coaches can customize the developmental sports scale to suit their particular context and the unique needs of their players. Consider the example in figure 3.3, noticing the modifications made to the template.

Sport:			
Topic or Position:			
Level:			
3.0	**In addition to 2.0 knowledge and skills, the player demonstrates deeper applications and fluency with skills.** For example: • • • • • • •		**Observations**
	2.5	Player exhibits all the score 2.0 components and some of the elite 3.0 components.	
2.0	**Expected player proficiencies** • • • • • • • **The player exhibits no major errors or omissions.**		
	1.5	Player exhibits all the score 1.0 components and some of the 2.0 components.	

1.0	**Player knows and demonstrates basic knowledge and skills:**
	 • Recognizes or recalls specific sport terminology, such as—
	   →
	   →
	   →
	
	 Simpler knowledge and skills:
	 •
	 •
	 •		

Source: Adapted from Marzano, 2006, 2010, 2017.

Figure 3.3: Sample customized developmental sports scale template.

*Visit **MarzanoResources.com/reproducibles** for a blank reproducible version of this figure.*

This customized version of the template includes the following.

- Space for the coach to note the sport, topic or position, and age level

- A column for coaches and players to record observations

- Adjusted scoring based on the rationale that it's rare for an athlete to fall far below the level 1.0 on a scale (In this case, the coach highlights the simpler content and skills that need attention and development based on the player's level of physical and emotional maturity.)

- Highlighted proficiency to better signify the expectations for coaches and players

- Intermediate scores at 1.5 and 2.5, as well as modified language to more accurately reflect the sport (These intermediate levels allow athletes and coaches to track subtle growth markers that may not make a full point on the scale.)

- Score 1.0 often uses descriptors to communicate how the player is approaching proficiency at 2.0 (In some cases, it is easier to clearly articulate basic skills with asset language. However, in other sports and scales, it's more difficult to accomplish this at the 1.0 level.)

- You may see a phrase like *lacks confidence* or words such as *incorrectly* or *rarely* in cases when the coach accurately communicates the player's need for improvement with deficit language. This level may also include statistics like the number of correct and incorrect passes. For example, a volleyball coach speaking to a player needing support in passing might say something like, "Your passing is inconsistent. During practice you made two of five passes to the setter. You need to reach more toward four of five passes to the setter to be more proficient in that skill." In some sports, like baseball, errors are not only a statistic coaches keep and reference for training but are also noted on the public scoreboard. So, recognizing those qualifiers at 1.0 will be important for coaches to define their expectations for players.

Using developmental sports scales helps you clarify your expectations for your players. It also assists you in noticing improvement—even in small increments. Such improvement is important for keeping players motivated. Be aware that coaches may emphasize some areas of the game more than others. Using developmental sports scales with qualifiers at 1.0 allows coaches to personalize their expectations.

To see this in a real-life context, take a look at two sample developmental sports scales a high school baseball coach might use with players (see figures 3.4, page 63, and 3.5, page 64). Notice how the scale is structured: it identifies the essential skills that constitute player proficiency at score 2.0, simpler content related to the criterion at score 1.0, and expert content beyond the essential skills at score 3.0. Figures 3.4 and 3.5 contain developmental sports scales a high school baseball coach uses to assess infielders on glove positioning and ball tracking, and positioning and making plays.

Area: Infielding			
Topic: Glove Positioning and Ball Tracking			
Level: High School			
3.0	**In addition to 2.0 knowledge and skills, the player demonstrates deeper applications and fluency with skills.** For example: • Adapts easily to various surfaces (dirt or turf) when placing glove and anticipating ball hops • Adjusts to weather and other field conditions for glove placement and ball tracking		**Observations**
	2.5	Player exhibits all the score 2.0 components and some of the elite 3.0 components.	
2.0	**Expected player proficiencies** • Early glove presentation • Relaxed glove presentation • No wasted movement of glove • Glove leads player to the ball • Hands out in front • Hands pushed through the ball hops • Consistent catching and receiving of ball in the same spot in glove • Funnels the ball to center of chest **The player exhibits no major errors or omissions.**		
	1.5	Player exhibits all the score 1.0 components and some of the 2.0 components.	
1.0	**Player knows and demonstrates basic knowledge and skills:** • Recognizes or recalls specific sport terminology, such as— → *glove presentation* → *hands pushed* → *funnels* **Simpler knowledge and skills:** • Late glove presentation • Tense glove presentation • Wasted movement of the glove before the ball arrives like shaking, twisting, and so on • Glove follows rather than leads the player's feet to the ball • Hands on knees rather than out front in ready position • Hands stop at the ball hops rather than pushing through • Inconsistently catching and receiving ball in various spots in the glove • Leaving the ball in front of player at or near the feet rather than funneling it to the center of the chest		

Figure 3.4: Baseball developmental sports scale assessing glove positioning and ball tracking.

Area: Infielding			
Topic: Positioning and Making Plays			
Level: High School			
3.0	**In addition to 2.0 knowledge and skills, the player demonstrates deeper applications and fluency with skills.** For example: • Adapts easily to various surfaces (dirt or turf) in positioning • Adjusts infield positioning based on player knowledge of batting team player tendencies • Leads and communicates pickoff plays with other infielders		**Observations**
	2.5	Player exhibits all the score 2.0 components and some of the elite 3.0 components.	
2.0	**Expected player proficiencies** • Awareness of opposing base runners • Knowledge of other infielder tendencies in positioning and who plays which balls • Adjusts positioning based on coach direction • Confidence in picking skills—player aware of the pitcher throwing back and moves into place accordingly • Works in concert with catcher to position pickoff plays • Knows foot-to-bag positioning for various runners **The player exhibits no major errors or omissions.**		
	1.5	Player exhibits all the score 1.0 components and some of the 2.0 components.	
1.0	**Player knows and demonstrates basic knowledge and skills:** • Recognizes or recalls specific sport terminology, such as— 　→ *foot to bag* 　→ *pickoff plays* 　→ *base runners* **Simpler knowledge and skills:** • Relies on coaching cues to be aware of opposing base runners and to throw the ball • Working toward understanding other teammate infielder tendencies in positioning and who plays which balls; focuses on gaining confidence when playing balls up the middle • Relies on coaching cues to gauge position based on batters rather than doing so independently • Picking off skills occur once in a while rather than consistently • Lacks confidence in knowledge, often seeking clarity about catcher and infielders during pickoff plays • Places the wrong foot on the bag		

Figure 3.5: Baseball developmental sports scale assessing positioning and making plays.

Notice the score 2.0 specifies the essential knowledge and skills in which the coach expects his high school athletes to be proficient. A player scoring at the 2.0 level implies that player has mastered the 1.0 components. A coach might choose to work with the terminology practice first, checking in with players about their learning of the basic terms common to this skill. If players demonstrate a solid understanding of the sport-specific terminology, the coach moves on to addressing practice and performance on the basic processes. In the case of figure 3.4 (page 63), this means early glove presentation, relaxed glove presentation, no wasted movement of glove, glove leads player to the ball, hands pushed through the ball hops, hands out in front, consistent catching and receiving of ball in the same spot in glove, and funnels the ball to center of chest.

When you create developmental sports scales, make sure the components at score 1.0 have a direct relationship with the score 2.0 learning targets. Each score 1.0 target most often builds to target at the score 2.0 level. So, you will see that the first target at the score 2.0 level is early glove presentation. Notice the first target for score 1.0 is also related to glove presentation. Typically, players master score 1.0 components before the coach assesses them at the score 2.0 level. Consequently, the levels of a developmental sports scale inform the sequence of practice. During practice, a coach might provide minilessons and repetition to the simpler knowledge and skills at score 1.0, observing this content to ensure players master them prior to instructing to score 2.0 components.

At score 3.0, the scale identifies a target that clearly exceeds the criterion at score 2.0 (Hoegh, Flygare, Heflebower, & Warrick, 2023). Here, the player exhibits increased fluidity, efficient applications, and consistent performance. Players who reach proficiency at the score 3.0 level often apply knowledge, skills, and intangibles to new contexts beyond those they have practiced, signaling new thinking, reasoning, and applications rather than simple recall. For instance, adjusting the glove work and hands from a natural dirt surface to turf or vice versa. It is important to note because score 3.0 indicates application beyond what the coach taught, players may demonstrate performance at this level in any number of ways, not just the target at score 3.0. For this reason, many developmental sports scales introduce the learning target at score 3.0 with the language, *In addition to 2.0 knowledge and skills, the player demonstrates deeper applications and fluency with skills.* Use the observations column to note how each player demonstrates skills at this level, providing adequate details and examples.

It should be clear from this discussion of developmental sports scales that the components called out at each level of the scale represent qualitative differences in player performance rather than quantitative differences. In other words, player performance at each level of the developmental sports scale will constitute a different degree of understanding as well as a consistency in execution (Heflebower, Hoegh, Warrick, & Flygare, 2019; Hoegh et al., 2023). For instance, using performance evidence to determine a player's thinking is significantly different at a score 1.0 task compared to a score 2.0 task. At score 3.0, players need to apply their score 2.0 knowledge or skills in a new situation, and thus the reasoning, fluidity, and performance is beyond the score 2.0 performance.

Also note that it is relatively easy to adjust scales for varying levels of athletes (from high school downward to middle school, or from high school upward to college). For example, if you slide the scale up by making the level 1.0 content the 2.0 content, and the 2.0 content for the 3.0 content, you have easily modified the high school scale to a lower level of expectation and maturity, like middle school. Here you would simply add a new set of 1.0 skills at a lower expectation based upon players' levels and ages. The same works for coaching college (or other elite programs): you may slide some of the targets on the scale down. Here, the 3.0 targets might become the expected 2.0 knowledge and skills, the 2.0 would slide down to become the 1.0 expectations, and you would draft new 3.0 expectations more indicative of the knowledge and skills expected at such higher levels.

Reflection

✳ **What aspects of the customized developmental sports scale would be most beneficial for your athletes?**

_____

_____

_____

_____

_____

_____

_____

✳ **What, if any, modifications should you use to suit your program or your athletes' needs?**

_____

_____

_____

_____

_____

_____

_____

✳ **What intangibles are important to generate a developmental sports scale to use with your athletes?**

_____

_____

_____

_____

_____

_____

_____

Determine What You Will Teach and Assess

PRACTICE SESSIONS PLANNING

Given that coaches can view the developmental sports scale as a skill and performance progression, identifying steps players will take in reaching the criterion at score 2.0, coaches can also use the scale as the basis of a practice plan. Consider the following tips for using developmental sports scales to plan practice sessions.

- **Start with a preassessment:** Conduct a preassessment to determine where most players begin their journey on the scale's progression. Using that data, coaches may begin emphasizing essential skills at score 1.0 in practice.

- **Divide information at the 1.0 level into small pieces:** Practices identify the target prerequisite information and skills at the 1.0 level and present this information in small chunks. Carefully but quickly present this preliminary information and practice drills to allow players to deepen this basic knowledge.

- **Allow players to advance as they achieve mastery:** Once players achieve performance representing score 1.0, they are ready for more rigorous lessons for the score 2.0 components, and so on through the developmental sports scale.

- **Make the scale a centerpiece of the practice session:** During practice, frequently refer to the levels of the developmental sports scales—especially when offering players feedback. This empowers players to self-assess and take ownership of their progress. It also cues players to see practices as opportunities to monitor their performance rather than just taking a moment to measure their success in a single practice or competition situation (Flygare et al., 2022).

- **Customize instruction:** If players do not consistently move toward mastery of one or more of the components at score 1.0, consider changing your practice strategies. For example, during a baseball drill, you realize while players are adept at relaxed glove placement, they are not pushing the hands through the hop of the ball as it comes into the body, causing less fluidity and the likelihood of dropped balls. You might design a reteaching lesson to solidify this component. Then, you would initiate an additional performance to ensure player understanding at the proper level for the retaught skill. You would not need to reevaluate the other score 1.0 components since the earlier performance indicated solid player understanding of those components.

- **Work with varying levels when appropriate:** It is possible during performance drills to represent every level of the developmental sports scale at score 1.0, score 2.0, and score 3.0 to provide players opportunities to demonstrate their highest ability for a specific skill component. If so, you must make some important decisions. Should coaches stop evaluating components once they see players master them in a competition? There are instances in which it makes sense to cease evaluating these components. When the components represent discrete pieces of knowledge or basic skills not essential later in the practice or competition situations, then coaches may choose to stop assessing once it is clear players have mastered them. More often, though, the opposite is true. Components coaches teach and evaluate early in practices are essential building blocks for later learning, either in the current practice or later ones. If players have mastered these early components, coaches are likely to continue assessing them later to ensure the knowledge or skill has not degraded.

The reproducible "Planning Practice Sessions" at the end of this chapter (page 73) provides a tool you can use to plan practices based on the information you gather from developmental sports scales. Developmental sports scales are versatile tools that serve as the hub for planning, practice, evaluation, and feedback. Figure 3.6 illustrates this relationship.

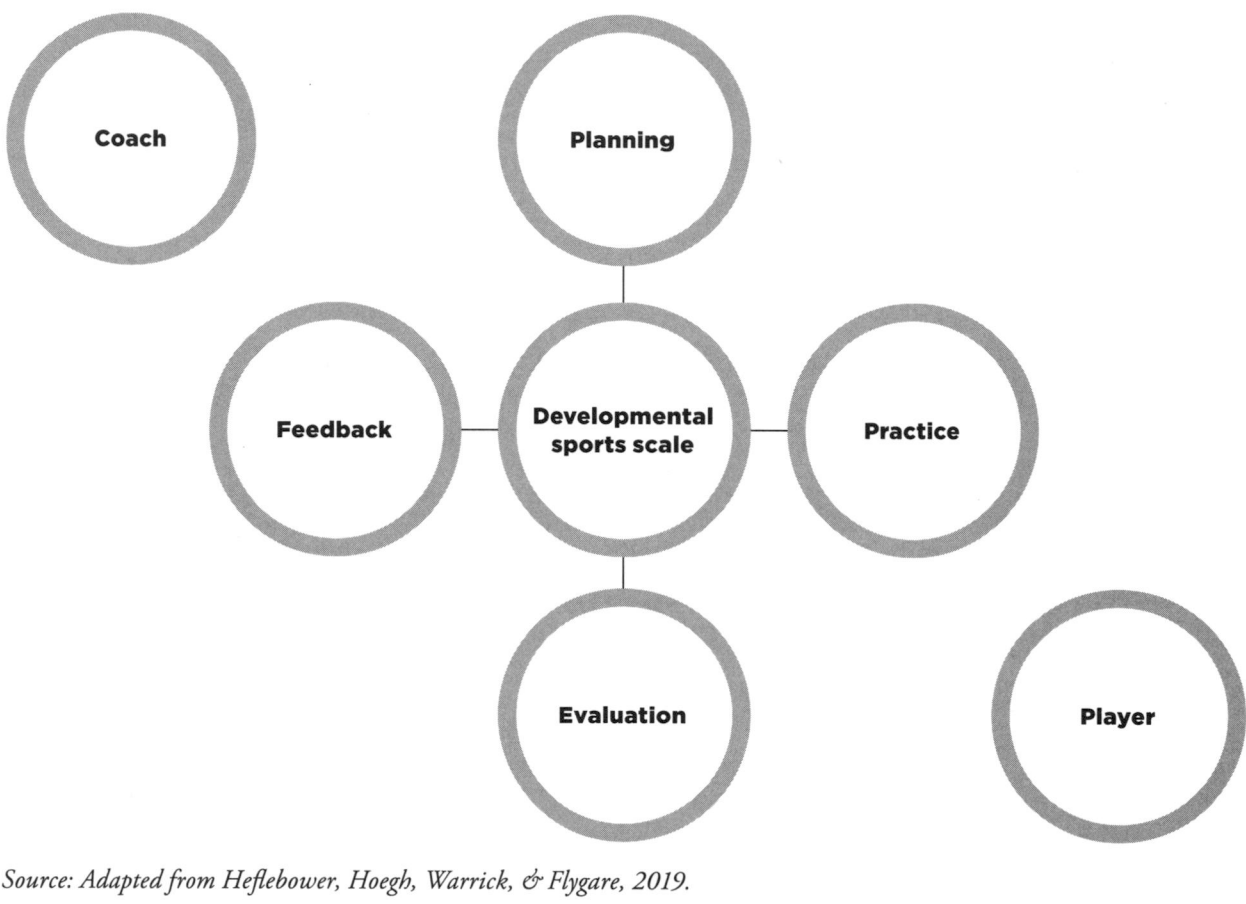

Source: Adapted from Heflebower, Hoegh, Warrick, & Flygare, 2019.

Figure 3.6: The role of the developmental sports scale in player development.

Notice how the developmental sports scale serves as the central document describing what happens in practice, and thus as a common point of understanding of the learning between coaches, players, and even parents and caregivers (when applicable).

Determine What You Will Teach and Assess

Reflection

PAUSE FOR A MOMENT TO REFLECT ON THE FOLLOWING QUESTIONS.

✳ **How will working with developmental sports scales change the way you plan practice sessions?**

_____

_____

_____

_____

_____

_____

✳ **How will this process change the way you focus on essential skills with players?**

_____

_____

_____

_____

_____

_____

✳ **Based on the graphic in figure 3.6 (page 68), how will developmental sports scales change your coaching practice?**

_____

_____

_____

_____

_____

_____

_____

Determine What You Will Teach and Assess

BENEFITS OF USING DEVELOPMENTAL SPORTS SCALES

There are some key benefits in using developmental sports scales you can expect to access quickly once you begin centering them in your work with athletes. As you share the developmental sports scales with players, they have the opportunity to set and monitor progress toward goals on their own. Periodic drills and performances serve as milestones to gauge how the learning is going for *both* the coach and the player! Although players will progress at different rates, all athletes will be progressing in measurable ways, offering opportunities to celebrate their progress. In this way, the priority knowledge, skills, and intangibles become the focus of their learning, and the scale serves as the vehicle by which that learning takes place. Both coach and players have a tangible tool for monitoring and assessing the players' progress toward proficiency.

Additionally, once they establish content of clear goals, coaches can then place the practice activities in that context. Players will understand how each practice drill and competition contributes to their journey to becoming better players. Further, identifying *long-term goals* (goals in operation for more than just a few practices) allows players to set personal achievement goals based on the developmental sports scales and then track their personal progress toward achieving the goals they set for themselves. This connects players personally and emotionally to those goals central to their development during practices and competitions. This is a powerful force of intrinsic motivation and will produce surprising benefits for players individually and the team collectively.

Due to the emotional involvement of players in their own learning and performance, they are more likely to work hard, complete drills, and positively take on performances because they want to understand the progress they are making on their personal goals. This creates a fundamental change in the way the sport operates. All players have their own goals based on the sport components. Achievement by one player does not always come at the cost of other players. In this way, athletes become more of a team, with the sense that "we are all in this together." When each player gets independently better, so does the team as a whole.

Another important change you can expect when players are tracking their personal progress on their goals is they will become more likely to take performance risks. Players often develop risk taking after they understand their own effort connects to improved progress. Tracking progress on personal goals helps players see this progress, especially if coaches take the time to review player progress on goals and find important ways to celebrate player success. All of this is possible when criteria help align practice goals, practice strategies, and performances.

Reflection

PAUSE FOR A MOMENT TO REFLECT ON THE FOLLOWING QUESTIONS.

* Which of these benefits is most exciting to you and would most benefit your team?

_____
_____
_____
_____
_____
_____
_____

* How might developmental sports scales boost your players' intrinsic motivation?

_____
_____
_____
_____
_____
_____
_____
_____
_____

* What is your first step in implementing the tools in this chapter?

_____
_____
_____
_____
_____
_____
_____
_____

Determine What You Will Teach and Assess

Summary

In this chapter, you learned how to adopt performance-based coaching. You read about a detailed process you can use to decide what knowledge and skills are essential for players to thrive in their sport. You encountered a template and a few examples of developmental sports scales that clearly delineate coaching expectations and learned options for customizing them to your particular context. As we alluded, learning a sport is a bit messy, but it shouldn't be a mystery. By clarifying the expectations for themselves, other staff members, and players, coaches prepare for increased player ownership and success. Taking the mystery out of the messiness will help you, your coaching staff, your players, and your entire team monitor and assess proficiency.

Planning Practice Sessions

Use the following chart to plan your practice session based on data you've gathered using your team's developmental sports scales. In the second column, note which knowledge, skills, and intangibles you will focus on during practice. In the third column, note which drills the team will use to practice them. And in the right-most column, note how you will group players during the drills. Finally, take notes and make reflections in the space provided during or after practice to help you in planning future practice sessions or when providing feedback for players in their developmental sports scales.

Sport and Team:			
Practice Date:			
	Knowledge, Skills, and Intangibles	**Drills**	**Players**
3.0			
2.0			
1.0			
Reflection:			

CHAPTER 4

Use Developmental Sports Scales for Tracking, Feedback, and Goal Setting

Much has been written about the idea of developmental sports scales (also called *proficiency level descriptors*, *scales*, or *proficiency scales*) through the lens of students in the classroom (Heflebower, 2005; Heflebower et al., 2014, Hoegh, Heflebower, & Warrick, 2020; Marzano, 2006), yet this is the first time using these developmental sports scales with athletes as a coaching tool. Therefore, coaches must consider the impact and importance of writing (or revising) sports scales, making time to use them with athletes, and reflecting on them while making coaching decisions. Coaches may use developmental sports scales multiple times in multiple ways.

In this chapter, we illustrate how coaches can use developmental sports scales early on to establish team expectations with players and their families. We also show how data from developmental sports scales are useful for progress tracking. Readers learn how to build reflection practices with players and establish routines for providing feedback. Coaches should strive to employ characteristics of quality feedback so it's targeted and effective for players to grow toward proficiency. Finally, we discuss how coaches and players work together to set goals so each player individually and as a member of the team collectively works toward peak performance.

Team Expectations

When is the best time to introduce developmental sports scales? As soon as possible! An essential part of beginning your work with a group of athletes is setting the vision and tone and communicating your expectations; bringing the developmental sports scales into this process is a natural fit. As we pointed out in chapter 3 (page 54), this is especially true of intangibles like attitude, effort, and participation.

Coach Logan Heflebower experienced this as a head baseball coach at a high school. At his first player meeting, Coach Heflebower shared two developmental sports scales (specifically for the intangibles he expected) with his players. Figure 4.1 offers a sample script demonstrating how a coach might introduce the concept of developmental sports scales at an early players meeting.

Use Developmental Sports Scales for Tracking, Feedback, and Goal Setting

> To ensure we are all clear on my expectations for participation and effort, I created these developmental sports scales. As our season progresses, we will use these scales to define and track expected baseball knowledge, skills, and intangible traits. We will stop periodically throughout our practices for you to look over the expectations and self-reflect. I will also use the sports scales to provide you with specific feedback and, ultimately, to decide playing time. When you have questions about your progress, refer to the sports scales. When you wonder about your progress or playing time, self-reflect. If your parents ask you about your positioning or playing time, refer to the developmental sports scales. There are really no coaching secrets. You must develop and perform these various skills. The more you reflect, improve, and master these skills, the more you play.

Figure 4.1: Sample script for introducing developmental sports scales to players.

Figure 4.2 shows a developmental sports scale similar to the one Coach Heflebower shared with his players, detailing expectations for participation and preparedness.

Sport:			
Topic: Expectations for Participation and Preparedness			
Level: High School			
3.0	**In addition to 2.0 knowledge and skills, the player demonstrates deeper applications and fluency with skills.**		**Observations**
	For example: • Demonstrates team leadership and involvement that exceed expectations, such as organizing the team for practice, actively assisting other players to help them understand, and so on • Focuses on the task exceeding expectations, such as being self-directed and having an enthusiastic attitude • Prepares to learn by arriving early to practice and consistently working hard • Exceeds deadlines and practice expectations by turning in reflections with honest and detailed information and holding self to a high standard		
	2.5	Player exhibits all the score 2.0 components and some of the elite 3.0 components.	
2.0	**Expected player proficiencies**		
	• Is actively involved in practice situations and discussions by sharing information and sometimes even performing a leadership role • Focuses on the practice task by working independently, self-adjusting, and exhibiting a positive attitude • Prepares to learn by being on time, bringing proper equipment, and showing up ready to work hard • Meets deadlines and practice expectations **The player exhibits no major errors or omissions.**		
	1.5	Player exhibits all the score 1.0 components and some of the 2.0 components.	
1.0	**Player knows and demonstrates basic knowledge and skills:**		

	• Recognizes or recalls specific sport terminology, such as—
	  → *leads during practice*
	  → *shows a positive attitude*
	  → *practice expectations*
	Simpler knowledge and skills:
	• Demonstrates reduced involvement in practice situations and requires prompts to participate, relies on the contributions of others, and struggles to initiate sharing information
	• Attends practice inconsistently; struggles to arrive on time, bring proper equipment, and be ready to work hard
	• Focuses on the task only with frequent reminders and relies on others to perform the drill or model techniques
	• Prepares to learn only with frequent reminders to be on time, bring equipment, and be ready to practice
	• Struggles to meet practice quality expectations, needing consistent reminders to review a skill and modify form
	• Demonstrates awareness of deadlines and practices quality expectations inconsistently; initiates arrangements with coach to address lateness or redo skills		

Figure 4.2: Expectations for participation and preparedness.

*Visit **MarzanoResources.com/reproducibles** for a blank reproducible version of this figure.*

Coach Heflebower provided time for players to reflect about the developmental sports scale after the first week of practice. He found players needed about ten minutes to review the text and another five minutes to write notes and observations while self-reflecting. Coach Heflebower waited until the Friday after the first week of practice to collect players' sports scales. He then took time to review them and consider how players' self-reflections aligned with what he'd observed during practice. This allowed players to take the reflection seriously, realizing their coach was observing them according to the expectations of the sports scale and providing feedback accordingly.

Coaches can use the following procedures to obtain player reflection and provide feedback.

1. Share an intangibles scale with players.

2. Ask players to independently read the score 2.0 content.

3. Invite a few players to share what the statements mean to them. The coach adds, refines, and redirects as needed.

4. Describe how you will use the developmental sports scales in practices (providing guidance to players, gaining feedback, and allowing players to practice reflection and set goals).

5. After one (or more) practice, ask players to reflect on their level of proficiency based on the statements in the developmental sports scale. Then, provide time for players to record their self-reflection in the Observations column (see figure 4.2, page 77).

6. Collect players' reflections and review them, adding notes of agreement or disagreement and providing key feedback for improvement. Coaching teams may want to divvy them up.

7. Return the updated developmental sports scales to each player and allow time for all players to consider the coach's feedback.

8. Periodically remind players how they should use developmental sports scales to track their progress and monitor their goals.

For a real-life example of this process, see the case study in chapter 5 (page 97).

Reflection

PAUSE FOR A MOMENT TO REFLECT ON THE FOLLOWING QUESTIONS.

✳ **What intangible skills are important in your sport?**

_____

_____

_____

_____

_____

_____

Use Developmental Sports Scales for Tracking, Feedback, and Goal Setting

✳ **When is the best time for you to introduce developmental sports scales to your athletes?**

_____

_____

_____

_____

_____

_____

_____

_____

✳ **Which scales would you share with players first? Essential knowledge and skills or intangibles?**

_____

_____

_____

_____

_____

_____

_____

_____

_____

Progress Tracking

Athletes tracking their own progress is a key component of an objective learning environment. It is also supported as effective in both research and practice (Fisher & Frey, 2012; Heflebower et al., 2019; Marzano, 2017).

Teaching players to track their progress using developmental sports scales empowers them to take ownership of monitoring their skill development and increasing their competency, thereby boosting intrinsic motivation. The coach will direct players each to denote where they are on the developmental sports scale. While this may be done on paper, many coaches opt to put this into an interactive online tool (like a Google Form or Google Doc) and send it from their phones at the end or right after practice.

Figure 4.3 (page 80) shows how one of Coach Heflebower's players responded to the scale, taking notes about his current proficiency level in the Observations column.

Sport: Baseball			
Topic: Expectations for Participation and Learning			
Level: High School			

3.0	**In addition to 2.0 knowledge and skills, the player demonstrates deeper applications and fluency with skills.**		**Observations**
	For example: • Demonstrates team leadership and involvement that exceed expectations, such as organizing the team for practice, actively assisting other players to help them understand, and so on • Focuses on the task exceeding expectations, such as being self-directed and having an enthusiastic attitude • Prepares to learn exceeding expectations by arriving early to practice and consistently working hard • Exceeds deadlines and practice expectations by turning in reflections with honest and detailed information and holding self to a high standard		• *Nope. Not here on most things.*
	2.5	Player exhibits all the score 2.0 components and some of the elite 3.0 components.	
2.0 * *	**Expected player proficiencies** • (Leads) and is actively involved in practice situations and discussions by sharing information and sometimes even performing a leadership role • Focuses on the practice task by working independently, self-adjusting, and exhibiting a positive attitude • Prepares to learn by being on time, bringing proper equipment, and being ready to work hard • Meets deadlines and practice expectations **The player exhibits no major errors or omissions.**		• *Not leading things.* • *I think my attitude is pretty positive most days.* • *I am meeting deadlines and working on this self-reflection thing.*
	1.5	Player exhibits all the score 1.0 components and some of the 2.0 components.	

1.0	**Player knows and demonstrates basic knowledge and skills:**
	 • Recognizes or recalls specific sport terminology, such as—
	   → *leads during practice*
	   → *shows a positive attitude*
	   → *practice expectations*
	 Simpler knowledge and skills:
	 • Demonstrates reduced involvement in practice situations; requires prompts to participate, relies on the contributions of others, and struggles to initiate sharing information
	 • Attends practice inconsistently; struggles to arrive on time, bring proper equipment, and be ready to work hard
	 ✓ • Focuses on the task only with frequent reminders and relies on others to perform the drill or model techniques
	 • Prepared to learn only with frequent reminders to be on time, bring equipment, and be ready to practice
	 ✓ • Struggles to meet practice quality expectations, needing consistent reminders to review a skill and modify form
	 ✓ • Demonstrates awareness of deadlines and practices quality expectations inconsistently; initiates arrangements with coach to address lateness or redo skills
			• *I do most of this stuff well. Except, I need to work on practice expectations—I need some reminders about my skills.*
			 • *I put a check mark next to those I need to work on more.*
			 • *I know what the terms all mean.*

Figure 4.3: Sample developmental sports scale including player self-assessment.

Use Developmental Sports Scales for Tracking, Feedback, and Goal Setting

In figure 4.3 notice the player placed check marks next to the score 1.0 skills that need more attention and made notes in the Observations column. Also, this player put a star next to those skills he thought he was doing consistently at this time. The player circled the word *leads* to indicate a proficiency he was not meeting and wished to focus on improving.

Another way players can work with developmental sports scales is using a highlighting system. Bring two different color highlighters to practice. Use one to represent *good to go*—those competencies players consistently illustrate. The other indicates those skills needing more attention.

Figure 4.4 shows how coaches and players use the highlighting system to give and respond to feedback. In this version of the developmental sports scale, the player used the darker highlighting to indicate competencies he believes he excels in and the lighter highlighting to indicate competencies he believes he still needs improvement in. The coach then responded to each player's self-assessment in the Observations column.

Area: Player Behavior		
Topic: Expectations for Participation and Effort		
3.0	In addition to score 2.0 knowledge and skills, the player demonstrates deeper applications and fluency with skills.	Observations
	• Demonstrates team leadership and involvement exceeding expectations, such as organizing the team for practice, actively assisting other players to help them understand, and so on • Focuses on exceeding expectations, such as being self-directed and having an enthusiastic attitude • Prepares to learn exceeding expectations by arriving early to practice and consistently working hard • Exceeds deadlines and practice expectations by turning in reflections with honest and detailed information and holding self to a high standard	• *I agree these aren't developed yet. I'm not as concerned about these, as they exceed my initial expectations.*
	2.5 Player exhibits all the score 2.0 components and some of the elite 3.0 components.	
2.0	**Expected player proficiencies** • Leads and is actively involved in practice situations and discussions by sharing information and sometimes even performing a leadership role • Focuses on the practice task by working independently, self-adjusting, and exhibiting a positive attitude • Prepares to learn by being on time, bringing proper equipment, and showing up ready to work hard • Meets deadlines and practice expectations **The student exhibits no major errors or omissions.**	• *I do see you actively involved in practices. I haven't noticed you leading drills either.* • *I must slightly disagree. I saw you mutter frustration when I asked you to redo a drill. That isn't the positive attitude I expect.* • *You have forgotten some part of your practice gear a couple times.* • *You are on time, but need to be a bit more efficient in moving from drill to drill.*

Figure 4.4: Sample developmental sports scale using highlighting.

continued →

	1.5	Player exhibits all the score 1.0 components and some of the 2.0 components.	
1.0		**Player knows and demonstrates basic knowledge and skills:** • Recognizes or recalls specific sport terminology, such as— → *leads during practice* → *shows a positive attitude* → *practice expectations* **Simpler knowledge and skills:** • Demonstrates reduced involvement in practice situations; requires prompts to participate, relies on the contributions of others, and struggles to initiate sharing information • Attends practice inconsistently; struggles to arrive on time, bring proper equipment, and be ready to work hard • Focuses on the task only with frequent reminders and relies on others to perform the drill or model techniques • Prepared to learn only with frequent reminders to be on time, bring equipment, and be ready to practice • Struggles to meet practice quality expectations, needing consistent reminders to review a skill and modify form • Demonstrates awareness of deadlines and practice quality expectations inconsistently; initiates arrangements with coach to address lateness or redo skills	• *See my previous notes.*

Coaches use developmental sports scales in the best way for themselves and their players. For example, some coaches allow players to work with scales independently the first few practices, opting not to collect them for review and feedback. The scale in figure 4.4 (page 81) demonstrates how coaches offer feedback when they do collect sports scales for review. However you choose to use sports scales with players, remember receiving feedback from coaches is extremely valuable for players and allows them to grow toward proficiency. Strive to provide feedback as early on as possible so your athletes can benefit from your observations. This is especially true if there is a discrepancy between a player's self-assessment and the coach's observations—provide ample time so the player has the opportunity to self-correct.

Any method you prefer works well for player self-reflection. The most important thing is to set a designated time for players to complete an honest reflection using the developmental sports scales. If providing written feedback becomes a bit too time intensive, a more efficient option is to record verbal feedback for player reflections. This is as simple as recording a verbal note on a smartphone and converting it to text, which you can copy and paste into the developmental sports scale. There is no one "right" way to do this. The only wrong way is *not* to periodically provide athletes each with some feedback about their self-reflections and your observations.

Some coaches may elect to extend the individual tracking to include team tracking as well. As the tracking process increases in sophistication, so does the time it takes. Figure 4.5 is an example of a team progress chart for behaviors. Use the same tool to track team knowledge and skills as well.

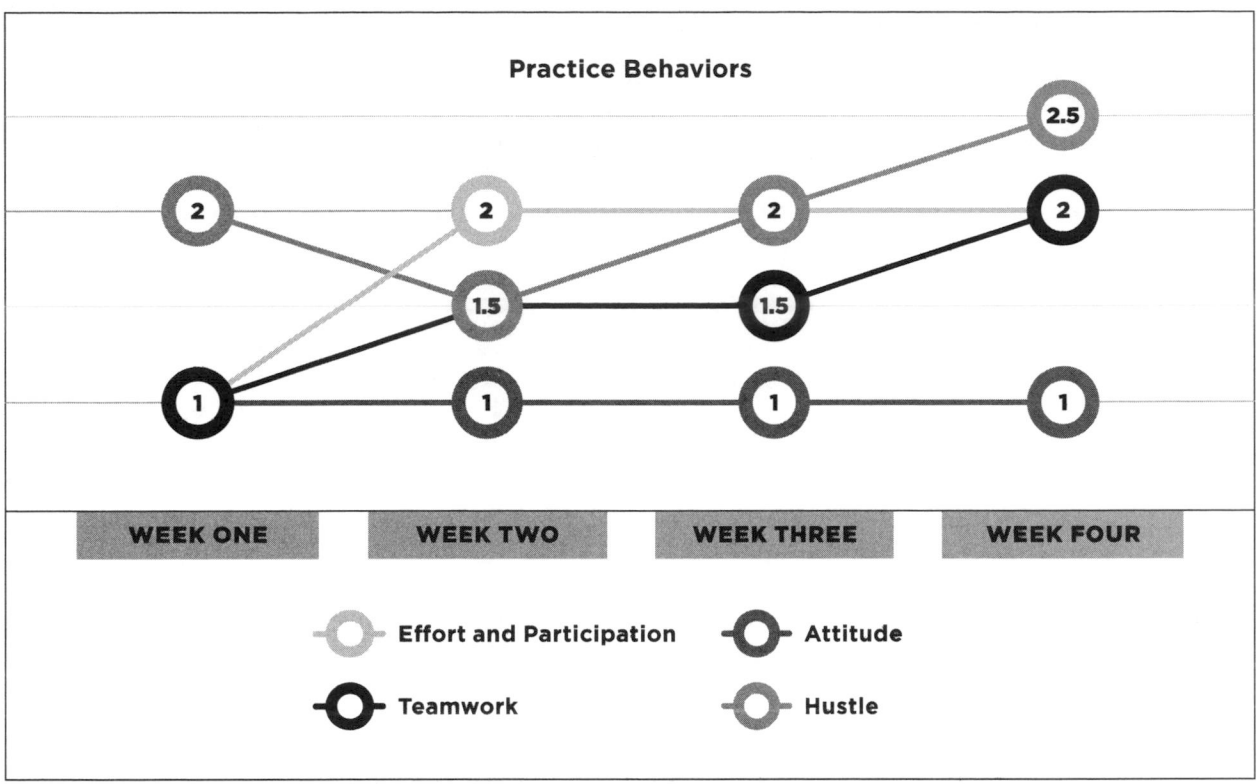

Source: Adapted from Heflebower et al., 2019.

Figure 4.5: Athletic team tracking form.

Notice tracking in this form not only offers players an awareness of how they are doing but also how their progress relates to their peers on the team. The coach simply reviewed the team on the behaviors of effort and participation, attitude, teamwork, and hustle. Now both the team and coaches are clear on areas of commendation—like the increase in effort and participation from 1.0 to 2.0—as well as areas in need of improvement—such as attitude, which is flatlined at 1.0. This provides focus for the coaches and the team. It also feels less subjective, because the coaches clearly outlined their expectations regarding intangible skills using the developmental sports scales. Much of the mystery is removed from statements like, "Hustle more!" or "Don't lose your head!" and specified as to what hustling looks like and what it means to exhibit a positive attitude.

Consider the following process to get started.

- Clearly outline the specific intangible skills you will measure.

- Reference and use the development sports scale for each intangible skill.

- Review each intangible skill. Score each player during a set period of time.

- Review the scores players obtained for each of the intangibles.

- Average the scores for each intangible by adding together each player's individual score, then dividing that total by the number of players scored. You may need to round to the nearest half point.

- Chart the average for each intangible skill to show graphically.

Reflection

PAUSE FOR A MOMENT TO REFLECT ON THE FOLLOWING QUESTIONS.

* Which method of player reflection and coach feedback would you prefer with your team? Why?

* How would you use the team-tracking idea in your program?

* Which skills should you track and how should you communicate the data to the coaching staff and players?

Use Developmental Sports Scales for Tracking, Feedback, and Goal Setting

Reflection Practices

How often will you use developmental sports scales with your athletes? Of course, this depends on the level of athletes you are coaching and how many new skills you are introducing. Be sure to make your use of the scales manageable.

Figure 4.6 shows how a coach schedules a two-week practice plan, embedding five reflection opportunities (indicated in boldface). Italicized text indicates times it might make sense for the coach to collect scales to review and provide feedback.

PRACTICE ONE
- Practice plan one
- **Player reflection one-to-one intangibles scale**

PRACTICE TWO
- Practice plan two

PRACTICE THREE
- Competition

PRACTICE FOUR
- Practice plan three
- **Player reflection two about the performance during the previous day's competition**

PRACTICE FIVE
- Practice plan four
- **Player reflection three about the same intangibles scale and two added sport-specific skill sports scales**
- *Coach collection one*

PRACTICE SIX
- Practice plan five
- Return reflection with coach's feedback

PRACTICE SEVEN
- Competition

PRACTICE EIGHT
- Practice plan six
- **Player reflection four about the performance during the previous day's competition**

PRACTICE NINE
- Practice plan seven

PRACTICE TEN
- Practice plan eight
- **Player reflection five**
- *Coach collection two*

Figure 4.6: Sample two-week practice plan with embedded reflection and feedback.

*Visit **MarzanoResources.com/reproducibles** for a blank reproducible version of this figure.*

What might the schedule look like during the preseason? Figure 4.7 shows a sample preseason two-week coaching plan. This is a preseason plan because there are two full weeks without a performance (game or match). This planning normally doesn't occur during the season in the same manner; rather, there are one or two performances embedded throughout any given week. It is possible to have multiple practices on one day, especially at the beginning of a season. In such cases, simply double the practice sessions. Notice there are six player reflection opportunities (indicated in boldface). The italicized text denotes two coach reflection collections.

PRACTICES ONE AND TWO
- Practice plan one
- Practice plan two
- **Player reflection one**

PRACTICES THREE AND FOUR
- Practice plan three
- Practice plan four

PRACTICES FIVE AND SIX
- Practice plan five
- Practice plan six
- **Player reflection two**

PRACTICES SEVEN AND EIGHT
- Practice plan seven
- Practice plan eight

PRACTICES NINE AND TEN
- Practice plan nine
- Practice plan ten
- **Player reflection three**
- *Coach collection one*

PRACTICES ELEVEN AND TWELVE
- Practice plan eleven
- Practice plan twelve
- Return reflection with coach's feedback.
- **Player reflection four**

PRACTICES THIRTEEN AND FOURTEEN
- Practice plan thirteen
- Practice plan fourteen

PRACTICES FIFTEEN AND SIXTEEN
- Practice plan fifteen
- Practice plan sixteen
- **Player reflection five**

PRACTICES SEVENTEEN AND EIGHTEEN
- Practice plan seventeen
- Practice plan eighteen

PRACTICES NINETEEN AND TWENTY
- Practice plan nineteen
- Practice plan twenty
- **Player reflection six**
- *Coach collection two*

Figure 4.7: Sample two-week preseason practice plan with multiple practices per day with embedded reflection and feedback.

*Visit **MarzanoResources.com/reproducibles** for a blank reproducible version of this figure.*

Use reflection more often early in the season, as the coaching team is establishing the culture and expectations. Increasing the reflection opportunities also helps shift extrinsic to intrinsic motivation—critical for effective players and teams (see chapter 2, page 34).

Reflection

PAUSE FOR A MOMENT TO REFLECT ON THE FOLLOWING QUESTIONS.

✳ **How might you embed time for player reflection into your practice schedule?**

_____

_____

_____

_____

_____

✳ **What challenges do you need to overcome to make this process effective and sustainable?**

_____

_____

_____

_____

_____

_____

✳ **When will you make time to provide feedback? What method works best for you?**

_____

_____

_____

_____

_____

_____

Use Developmental Sports Scales for Tracking, Feedback, and Goal Setting

Characteristics of Quality Feedback

Providing feedback to athletes is imperative. It goes hand in hand with players tracking their own progress and setting goals for themselves. Much has been written about players tracking progress, setting goals, and receiving quality feedback in the classroom and other educational environments (Brookhart, 2008; Heflebower, Hoegh, & Warrick, 2021; Heflebower et al., 2019; Hoegh et al., 2023; Marzano, Norford, Finn, & Finn, 2017).

Providing feedback using developmental sports scales is paramount for helping players know and be an integral part of their own performance as well. Hoegh and colleagues (2023) explained it this way:

> High-quality feedback is an essential part of the learning process, and done well, it has a notable impact. . . . Effective feedback is information provided to complement, enhance, augment, or in some way respond to or improve performance. Sufficient and effective feedback is more about quality than quantity. (p. 117)

Players rely on quality feedback to improve proficiency in their sport. When coaches offer feedback that is specific, timely, based on a predetermined set of criteria, and understandable to athletes at their development level, players have the information they need to adjust their performance. Feedback done well is unmatched in athletes' improvements. Duquesne University professor emerita Susan M. Brookhart's (2017) advice about feedback in the classroom holds true for athletes: "Effective feedback is part of a classroom assessment environment in which students see constructive criticism as a good thing and understand that learning cannot occur without practice" (p. 9). Effective feedback offers players valuable information that allows them to improve their performance.

How can coaches ensure they're offering high-quality feedback that will be effective for players to use and improve? In *Assessing Learning in the Standards-Based Classroom*, Hoegh and colleagues (2023) identify key characteristics of meaningful feedback, including specificity, tone, timeliness, amount, and comparison to criteria. We adapted them for high-quality coach feedback in the context of competitive sports as follows.

- **Specificity:** The coach should provide detailed written or spoken feedback in a way that players will understand. Consider a statement like, "When you're running to first base, exaggerate the pump of your arms, as it will help your legs speed up." Because the feedback is specific and detailed, the player knows what to do differently. *Specificity* means going beyond surface-level comments like, "You need to do better." Offer players specific and detailed feedback so they know what to do to be successful, rather than assuming they know what you mean.

- **Tone:** Monitor the tone you use with players to ensure it is honest, supportive, and kind. Coaches sometimes use humor or sarcasm to connect with players. While this might be appropriate in a relationship, it's not an effective choice for coach feedback. Consider how players will receive your feedback and be sure to provide actionable guidance rather than being overly critical. This might require you to invest more time in the beginning, but you'll quickly adjust and the results are worth the investment. Put yourself in your players' shoes by remembering a time you received overly critical feedback. How did your body respond? Likely, your brain's emotional limbic system flared up, and may have confabulated the feedback details in such a way to make you perceive it differently from what the coach intended.

Brookhart (2008) notes, "Tone can inspire or discourage. It's important to choose words that imply players are agents, active learners—the captains of their own ship of learning, as it were" (p. 34). Do you want to inspire or discourage? Which supports intrinsic motivation? This does not mean holding back on your feedback. You should be honest. It does means choosing a supportive tone tailored toward each player's intrinsic motivation. If you're unsure if you've accomplished this, have a quick conversation with your athletes after practice to ensure they have interpreted the feedback as you intended.

- **Timeliness:** *When* coaches offer feedback to players is important. If you wait long after the play or series is complete, the teachable moment may have passed. Provide feedback as close to the situation as possible. The amount of time between the activity and the feedback has a critical effect on player performance. The longer the delay in giving feedback, the less likely players will respond to the feedback and the less likely their performance will be enhanced (Bangert-Drowns, Kulik, Kulik, & Morgan, 1991; Stronge, 2018). Equally important is to ensure players have time to grapple with their skills a bit during early attempts. Assessment expert and best-selling author Dylan Wiliam (2018) noted "if it [feedback] is given too early, before students have had a chance to work on a problem, then they will learn less" (p. 127). This applies to athletes too. One way to do this is to ask more questions during the early part of the practice. An example might be, "What were you thinking when you passed cross-pitch and beyond three players closer to you?" The player now is thinking about what just happened, processing it, and engaging in solving the issue. If the coach always jumps in with only corrective suggestions, players don't have time to be integrally involved in making the improvements.

Finally, make sure players have time to react to the feedback prior to the next practice or competition. Feedback about a final game offers no chance for implementation. Instead, offer feedback, model proficiency, and then ask the player to perform five to ten of the corrected procedures or skills. This correction with repetitive practice offers the player time to use the skill so accurate practice becomes permanent. Allow players to use the feedback you provide and adjust their performance accordingly.

- **Amount:** Players logistically can't accommodate feedback on every aspect of performance. Coaches must be discerning about how much feedback a player can accommodate at any given time. Select a couple of main points to comment on. Ask yourself, "What is the most egregious error warranting feedback? Is it the footwork, ball contact, or follow-through?" Thinking in terms of the essential skills you identified in the developmental sports scales can help with this process—it's about narrowing focus.

If you're unsure how to start, look for patterns in player errors (Fisher & Frey, 2012). For example, if a baseball player continues to have incorrect glove placement, try to determine what understanding the player is missing. Does the player lack the connection between glove placement and a ball going underneath it? What is the pattern? By focusing on the bigger errors, you can offer specific feedback about understanding, rather than noting single errors after every single performance during a drill. Oftentimes, this is where meeting with small groups of players who make similar pattern errors is a more effective use of your time and resources. Giving feedback in a small-group setting prevents the coach from correcting each player independently, maximizing time and resources. Additionally, coaches can give general feedback to the team on its whole performance relative to the proficiency scale.

- **Comparison to criteria:** Returning to developmental sports scales will ensure your feedback aligns with your team's essential knowledge, skills, and intangibles. Structure feedback in a way that refers players back to the proficiency criteria. As tempting as it is, refrain from comparing players to one another! Let your sports scales serve as the objective standard. When coaches single out athletes, it can cause implicit comparisons and foster more angst than teamwork. Compare athletes to themselves or to a set of criteria for the best results. The effect is players each competing only against themselves to be their best. If players have set personal goals for their journey up the sports scale, they will view the coach's feedback as useful to them in working toward their goal. Further, players who are aware of their current level on the proficiency scale, the next level they are striving to achieve, or both, will more likely see the coach's comments in the content of the levels, better equipping those players to apply feedback in a game situation.

Reflection

PAUSE FOR A MOMENT TO REFLECT ON THE FOLLOWING QUESTIONS.

* **Does your approach to feedback include the key characteristics in this section?**

✳ **Which characteristics are you doing well with? Which ones need improvement?**

_____

_____

_____

_____

_____

_____

_____

_____

_____

✳ **What steps can you take to improve your approach to giving players feedback?**

_____

_____

_____

_____

_____

_____

_____

_____

_____

_____

Goal Setting

Giving quality feedback and goal setting go together. When coaches provide actionable feedback to players, they, in turn, can set goals to improve specific parts of their game. When coaches infuse goal setting as part of their everyday practice, players see how their individual improvement affects the overall performance of their teammates and team overall.

Goal setting works in tandem with feedback and tracking progress. As Heflebower and colleagues (2019) suggest, there are three components that increase the usefulness of goal setting in the classroom: (1) model goal setting, (2) explicitly teach the goal-setting process, and (3) provide strategies to help students obtain the goal.

What does this look like for coaches and players working with developmental sports scales? When modeling goal setting, think about how you approached the process in your personal or professional life, or recall a time you used goal setting as a former athlete and share that as an example for players. For example, say a coach tells players about a time he wanted to become a better hitter, so he set a batting average goal of over .300 in the next season. The coach explains to do that, he took at least one hundred swings three times a week in the offseason, videotaped a sample of swings, reviewed the sample swings, and focused on different tactics during the next session. For instance, one session's focus was on power. The next on quick hands, and so on.

As coauthors Connie M. Moss and Susan M. Brookhart (2009) explained, "Goal setting is more effective when 'guided' by three core questions for players: Where am I going? Where am I now? What strategy or strategies will help me get to where I need to go?" (p. 61). Using developmental sports scales specifies just that. These scales clearly help your athletes see where you want them to be (at the proficient level), where they are now, and then work with you on strategies to get them to the next level.

Consider the following process for incorporating goal setting into your practice.

- Use developmental sports scales as a reference point.

- Include a scale for intangibles as well as for sport-specific knowledge and skills.

- Ask players each to reflect on their performance on one or more scales.

- Provide players with your timely feedback.

- Require players to use their self-reflection with your feedback to develop a goal.

- Discuss how setting a goal requires a specific set of strategies to obtain it. These might include more specific practice, positive self-talk, or increasing strength.

- Teach players how to write a specific goal that includes what they will do, how they will accomplish it, and whether or not their strategies worked. Some coaches like to include possible limitations to this goal (time, availability of equipment, and so on) and ways the player may overcome such limitations.

- Use the goals by having athletes reference them, revise them, and celebrate accomplishing them.

This tool uses *SMART goals*, meaning they are strategic and specific, measurable, attainable, results oriented, and time bound. SMART goals—which coauthors George T. Doran, Arthur Miller, and James Cunningham developed (as cited in Doran, 1981)—ensure the goals athletes set are specific and ambitious enough to motivate them, while still being attainable in a reasonable time frame. See figure 4.8 for a template to use when setting SMART goals.

SMART Goal Areas	Athlete Application	Athlete Evidence and Reflection	Coach Review and Feedback
Strategic and specific (What is the goal? Be specific. Use language from the developmental sports scale.)			
Measurable (How will you measure your goal?)			
Attainable (Is this goal something you can likely attain?)			
Results oriented (What result will you accept as attainment of the goal?)			
Time bound (How long will this goal last? When will you review and revise it?)			

Source: Adapted from Heflebower et al., 2019.

Figure 4.8: Template for setting SMART goals.

*Visit **MarzanoResources.com/reproducibles** for a blank reproducible version of this figure.*

See the reproducible "Setting SMART Goals" (page 96) for a tool players can use to record and monitor their goals.

Players who use the developmental sports scales for goal setting will naturally answer three questions: Where am I going? Where am I now? What strategies will help me get to where I need to go? They can easily identify their destination and starting point using the scale's scoring system, as well as their self-reflection and the coach's feedback. Players will have specific ideas on how to arrive at the goal by referencing the components in the scale level they want to obtain.

Reflection

PAUSE FOR A MOMENT TO REFLECT ON THE FOLLOWING QUESTIONS.

* **Have you explicitly communicated a goal-setting process to athletes in your program? What is that process?**

_____

_____

_____

_____

_____

_____

_____

_____

* **If not, how would players individually and the team collectively benefit from setting goals and monitoring progress toward achieving them?**

_____

_____

_____

_____

_____

_____

_____

_____

Use Developmental Sports Scales for Tracking, Feedback, and Goal Setting

✳ **What role will the developmental sports scales play in the goal-setting process?**

_____

_____

_____

_____

_____

_____

_____

_____

_____

_____

_____

Summary

Developmental sports scales are a powerful tool not only for students in the classroom but also for players in competitive sports. Coaches must consider the impact and importance of writing or revising sports scales, making time to use them with athletes, and reflecting on them while making coaching decisions. Coaches may use developmental sports scales multiple times and in multiple ways. This chapter offered guidance about how to use developmental sports scales early on to establish team expectations with players and their families, and to track player and team progress. Additionally, it illustrated how to build reflection practices with players and establish routines for providing feedback. You encountered different options for considering how and when to use the scales with your athletes (during practice, after performances, and when you may want to collect them and share your own perspectives with your athletes). Remember to provide quality feedback tailored to help players grow toward proficiency. Finally, use the tools provided in this chapter to support players to set goals that guide them toward peak performance.

Setting SMART Goals

Review with players what SMART goals are and provide them with a copy of the following SMART goals worksheet. Players use the worksheet to construct a SMART goal that will support them to reach proficiency in an area they scored low on in the developmental sports scale. Players should use the space under the My Notes column to monitor their progress and take notes.

My Goal	Strategies I Will Try	My Timeline	My Progress	My Notes

Source: Adapted from Heflebower et al., 2019.

CHAPTER 5

Case Study and Experiential Vignette of Coach Heflebower's Players

Now that we've covered the foundational aspects of using developmental sports scales, in this chapter, we'll show what it looks like to use them in real-world contexts. Up to this point, we have discussed what is important to identify as critical knowledge, skills, and intangibles for your sport, as well as how to articulate your expectations using developmental sports scales. We also provided ideas for using the scales with your athletes to help them self-monitor and for you to provide more specific and effective feedback to your players.

In this chapter, we offer a case study and an experiential vignette that bring all the elements together to show you how they function in real-life settings. Coach Heflebower shares background details about how he used developmental sports scales with college athletes before introducing the specifics of the case study. Toward the end of the chapter, Coach Heflebower details his experiences in an experiential vignette at the high school level.

Collegiate Case Study

Although we wrote this book with a focus on coaching competitive sports at the middle and high school levels, coaches can successfully implement them at the college level. To prepare to study this approach with college athletes, Coach Heflebower read and reviewed specifically how to determine the prioritized criteria for infielders in collegiate baseball. He determined three topics of focus—(1) glove work and hands, (2) eyes and ball tracking, and (3) footwork and range—and wrote a developmental sports scale for each topic to use with his players. See appendix B (page 117) to view those developmental sports scales. Additionally, he worked to employ the strategies from chapter 4 (page 75) regarding feedback (specifically timeliness, specificity, tone, and connected to criteria), and asked players to reflect and set goals.

Coach Heflebower completed this case study with a NCAA Division II collegiate baseball team composed of a small group of ten athletes during a three-week preseason evaluation and reflection period in the fall of 2022. His goal was to have players record, analyze, and develop their skill-development progress via self-assessment. To do so, Coach Heflebower used the developmental sports scales to identify each player's areas of need. He used goal-setting language, as players could easily relate to the idea of setting a goal and using specific strategies to attain the goal. Players each were instructed to pick a weekly fundamental development goal (based on a component from their sports scale) and identify two or three specific strategies to help them work toward attaining the proficiency scale components within the weekly goal. Note the addition of detailing specific strategies to help athletes attain the components in a developmental sports scale.

Players received the following instructions:

> Pick a part of your infield game that we've established needs to improve, making sure you know why it needs to improve. Establish a *what*, *how*, and *why* process for analyzing that goal. Specifically, ask yourselves:
>
> - "What am I focused on this week?"
> - "How am I going to use my practice time to focus on this, and how do I tangibly work on this specific fundamental?"
> - "Why do I feel that I need improvement here?"
> - "Why is this important to my success as an infielder?"
>
> Then, list two or three ways in which your daily habits, drills (from those Coach Heflebower provided to you), mindset, and so on will benefit you working toward this goal you have established for the week.

METHOD

During this study, the infield coach monitored ten NCAA Division II collegiate baseball players for a three-week evaluation and reflection period during fall 2022 preseason practices. All infield players recorded, analyzed, received feedback, and used the information for self-assessment and development. They did so on the three developmental sports scale components the infield coach determined. Those components were: (1) glove work and hands; (2) eyes and ball tracking; and (3) footwork and range. Each infield player selected a weekly fundamental development goal, as well as two to three specific strategies to help them work toward proficiency in the weekly goal. (See the Findings section for examples from two players.)

Coach Heflebower developed the following goal-implementation process.

1. **Implement:** Implement the goal in *what*, *how*, and *why* format. What is your current status? How will you monitor your performance to improve? Why is this goal for improvement necessary? Each player presented this information in writing to the infield coach.

2. **Adjust:** Adjust your attention and skills. Monitor your efforts toward improvement of the specified goal you selected.

3. **Reflect:** At the end of the week, players each reflected about their progress toward the goal. What worked? What didn't?

4. **Review:** Players each determined if they mastered, almost mastered, or still needed to work on the skill. Players each rated themselves on a scale from 1 to 3 (with 1 being not successful or proficient and still needs to work on these components; 2 being partially proficient, getting there but not mastered, and still needing intrinsic or extrinsic cues from themselves or the coach; and 3 being mastered this skill). There is no need for cueing for players to be successful. This process is now a habit. These steps are similar to the developmental scale scores but were slightly modified to meet the needs of the coach and his players.

The premise was that each player used the previously mentioned essential skills and developmental sports scales to implement a goal. Players formally reflected three times about the most recent performance at practices or scrimmages. After each reflection, players each adjusted their performance based on personal reflections as well as three feedback responses from each player's position coach. During that reflection, players each scored themselves at that point in time.

Each week, the coach read each player's analysis about his specific goal and then provided written or verbal feedback connected to the player's goal. The coach presented the reflections to the player so each player could see how his reflection aligned with the coach's feedback. These reflections were directly connected to the coach's expectations on the essential skills and the corresponding developmental sports scales so players could make adjustments accordingly.

During this three-week study, all players were able to establish points of necessary growth for specific fundamentals unique to their levels and style of play. The following reflections were examples of the progress of self-reflection, as well as the development of skills through understanding the importance of details during self-reflection and assessment. Please note this case study does not include names, images, or likenesses of any players. All players contributed their artifacts anonymously. The two players' reflections and their corresponding coach's feedback are detailed in the findings.

FINDINGS

In this first case study, Coach Heflebower worked with two middle infielders. Each asked to use the developmental sports scales to create an individualized plan for reflection and goal setting.

Player One: Middle Infielder (Shortstop and Second Baseman)

During the first week, player one wrote an initial reflection document and shared it with Coach Heflebower. Figure 5.1 shows player one's reflection.

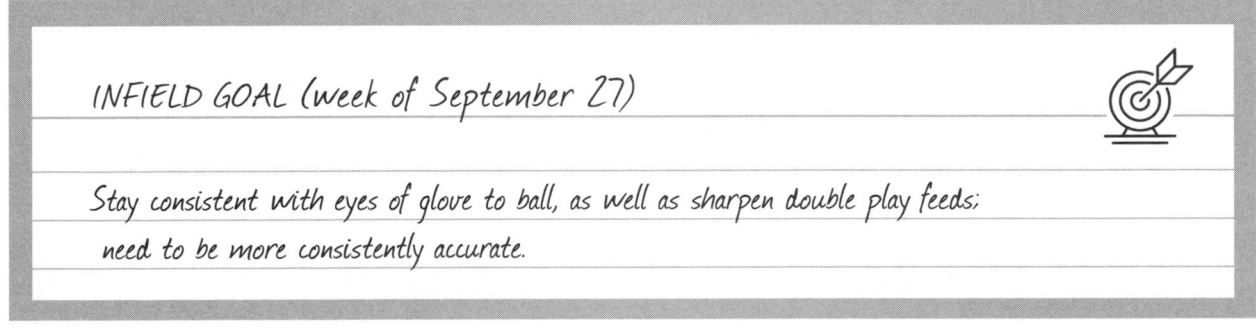

INFIELD GOAL (week of September 27)

Stay consistent with eyes of glove to ball, as well as sharpen double play feeds; need to be more consistently accurate.

Figure 5.1: Week one player one reflection.

Player one's initial goal lacked details as to the *what, how,* and *why* portion of the goal-setting process. Rather, his reflection included only a basic description with little regard to details that would lead to development. Player one scored his success for the week as a 1.5 (not successful or proficient, still needs work on this goal).

Note player one did reference two of the three essential skills as part of the process during his reflection during the week of September 27, 2022: *consistency of his eyes of glove to the ball,* as well as the *handwork for feeds for double plays.* These relate directly to the essential skills Coach Heflebower identified: *glove work and hands* and *eyes and ball tracking.* It is evident this player connected his performance to the coach's established essential skills.

Figure 5.2 shows Coach Heflebower's written feedback to player one.

GLAD YOU'RE RECOGNIZING THE IMPORTANCE OF CONSISTENCY.
WE NEED TO SEE IF WE CAN WORK ON A HOW AND WHY.

HOW ARE YOU GOING TO STAY CONSISTENT?
DO YOU NEED A PLAN, OR DO YOU ALREADY HAVE A PLAN?

WHY ARE WE SHARPENING DOUBLE PLAY FEEDS? AND HOW WILL WE DO THAT?
MORE SPECIFICITY IS GOING TO BE IMPORTANT FOR US HERE.

Figure 5.2: Week one coach feedback for player one.

In his week one feedback, Coach Heflebower explained while a broad goal is important, details are necessary to enhance developmental focus on the particulars that will lead to the success of the larger scale goal.

Figure 5.3 shows the reflection player one wrote during the second week.

INFIELD GOAL (week of October 3)

Better in my prep step: After the third inning or so, I found myself getting lazy with my prep step. Need to find consistency in my prep step being on time. My key is going to have to be a mental lock-in, if I'm more locked in on my prep step, my mental lock-in will be better elsewhere too (such as at the plate).

Figure 5.3: Week two player one reflection.

Notice the improvement. Player one was able to write a more robust goal by adding details and identifying *how* he would focus on improving. Initially, the finer details were lacking in the *how* portion of the goal setting of the reflection cycle. Player one improved in the identification of the strategies portion from the first week to the next by referencing the developmental sports scale components. He recognized that he needed a mental lock-in, a cue to sharpen his focus back to the task at hand. Although this second reflection improved on the first, this player still needed to add details about the small processes in tangible aspects of practice to build toward the larger goal. Player one rated himself for this week at 1.0 (partially proficient, getting there, but not mastered, still needing intrinsic or extrinsic cues from himself or the coach).

Figure 5.4 shows Coach Heflebower's feedback to the player's second week reflection.

GREAT THAT YOU'RE NOTING WHERE TO FOCUS.

CONSISTENCY IS A GREAT GOAL.
IS THERE A SPECIFIC PART OF PRACTICE YOU CAN PLAN TO WORK ON THIS?

FOR YOUR MENTAL CUE, THAT'S GREAT TO HAVE. WHAT WILL YOU TELL YOURSELF?
IS THERE A SPECIFIC CUE THAT WORKED BEST OR BETTER THAN OTHERS?

Figure 5.4: Week two coach feedback.

Notice the feedback explained the need for player one to add details in the process of the *how*, so it would be easier to track and establish tangible success.

Figure 5.5 shows the reflection player one wrote during the third week.

INFIELD GOAL (week of October 10)

Better in my approach to ground balls and post-throws. I'm finding myself getting in-between hops because I am not charging the ball. Work on taking away that unneeded hop and get the hop I want with better feet. For post-throw, I have to stop being stationary, I need to follow my throw.

Figure 5.5: Week three player one reflection.

Notice the continued improvement. In week three, player one went into detail about what specific parts of his game needed work. He used some of the language noted on the developmental sports scale. The reflection helped player one personalize his practices toward the prioritized criteria. It also helped player one more objectively see how important it is to practice drills and expectations, as well as how Coach Heflebower responded to him about his goal during practice. However, player one still lacked concrete details on tangible drills and fundamentals that would lead to success.

Player one rated himself this third week at 1.0 (partially proficient, getting there, but not mastered, still needing intrinsic or extrinsic cues from himself or the coach). The self-assessment was the same as his score in week two, but that is not uncommon. In fact, you may find your players hover at the 1.0 content and skills for a while, especially early in the season. The good news is, player one's goal got progressively more detailed. When players reflect and coaches provide detailed feedback, development happens! Coach Heflebower was fine-tuning his feedback as well. When coaches know what skills players are focusing on, their feedback is more specific and based on criteria.

Figure 5.6 shows Coach Heflebower's feedback to the player's third week reflection.

This player was a prime example of what you may also notice in some of your more developed and physically advanced athletes. They are physically very gifted, and mentally sound in their confidence of their abilities. However, they lack the ability to put their mechanics into words. They might say something simple like "I just fixed my feet because I wasn't getting it right." This blanket statement often comes from players who have strong fundamentals but struggle to encompass all the self-assessment and correction that goes on for them mentally during a couple reps from failure to success. It can also be difficult for coaches to coax this verbalization from players. However, when using developmental sports scales, the skills are specified, and the sport language is there (at score 1.0) to help players articulate it. This self-assessment is so important! However, it can often be a challenge for a coach. Yet when the coach clarified the skills and expectations ahead of time, paired with player reflection and coaching feedback all connected to the developmental sports scales, clarity and progress resound. These practices help coaches of even more elite athletes recognize and work toward more objective and purposeful player development.

LOVE THAT YOU'RE IDENTIFYING THE RESULT OF SOMETHING YOU NEED TO FIX → THE "BAD HOPS."

GREAT PLAN FOR FOLLOWING YOUR THROWS (THIS IS HARD FOR A TWO-WAY GUY, SINCE PITCHERS DON'T FOLLOW LIKE INFIELD GUYS DO).

ALSO LIKE THAT YOU'RE RECOGNIZING YOU NEED TO WORK INTO HOPS MORE AGGRESSIVELY TO GET EASIER HOPS.

THE AGGRESSOR ALWAYS WINS!

Figure 5.6: Week three coach feedback.

Player Two: Corner Infielder (First Baseman)

During week one, player two's initial reflection and goal statements started with suitable details in the *what*, *how*, and *why* of the reflection and goal-setting cycle.

Figure 5.7 shows player two's initial reflection, describing where in practice drills there were opportunities to make adjustments.

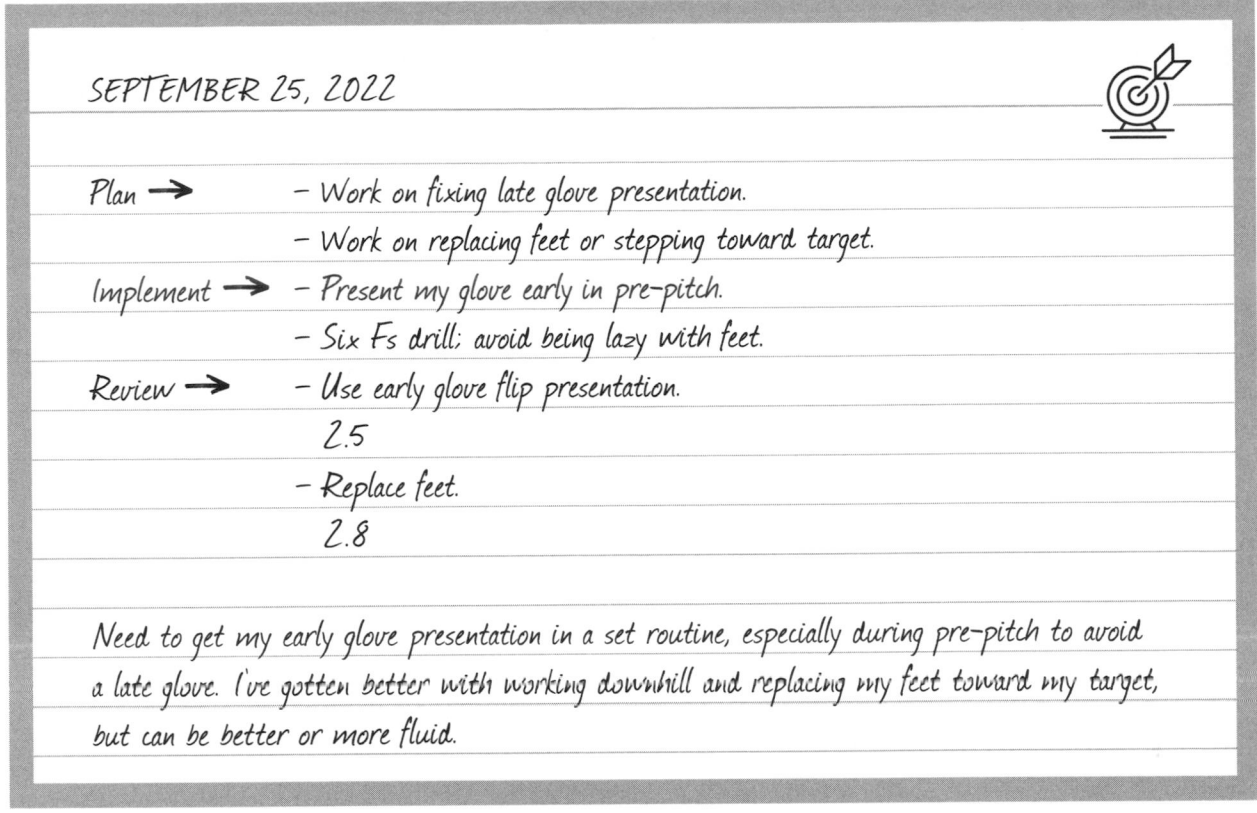

SEPTEMBER 25, 2022

Plan →   – Work on fixing late glove presentation.
              – Work on replacing feet or stepping toward target.
Implement →   – Present my glove early in pre-pitch.
              – Six Fs drill; avoid being lazy with feet.
Review →   – Use early glove flip presentation.
              2.5
              – Replace feet.
              2.8

Need to get my early glove presentation in a set routine, especially during pre-pitch to avoid a late glove. I've gotten better with working downhill and replacing my feet toward my target, but can be better or more fluid.

Figure 5.7: Week one player two reflection.

Player two rated his goal success for the week at 1.5 (partially proficient, getting there, but not mastered, still needing intrinsic or extrinsic cues from himself or the coach). Notice he recognized his need to present his glove early and avoid being lazy with his feet during the six Fs drill—practicing fielding a ground ball focusing on single word cues (feet, field, funnel, footwork, fire, follow) to help the player remember each part of the process.

At Coach Heflebower's first feedback opportunity, he discussed the importance of identifying the details of where the work can be done, specifically for the fundamentals in mind. Figure 5.8 shows his feedback.

GOOD DIRECT GOAL AND PLAN.

→ WITHIN DAILY DRILLS, THE GOAL OF FINDING COMFORT IN THE FUNDAMENTALS IS GREAT OR EASY WAY TO SEE IF YOU'RE DOING IT RIGHT.

IDENTIFYING YOU NEED TO FIND THE COMFORTABLE GLOVE EXTENSION IS GREAT—NOW YOU CAN ALWAYS CHECK YOURSELF ON IT BECAUSE YOU HAVE THAT FEEL.

Figure 5.8: Week one player two coach feedback one.

Notice the ways Coach Heflebower used the feedback strategies we discussed in chapter 4 (page 88). He exemplified specificity by making his comments detailed; the tone is illustrated using compliments and targeted advice—intended to make the player think and be invested; the coach was mindful of the amount of feedback—keeping his comments limited and focused; the appropriate amount of feedback was denoted in his brief comments focused on a couple of key areas; and he used related criteria by connecting feedback comments toward the developmental sports scales (see figure 5.7, page 103).

Figure 5.9 shows player two's week two reflection, which mentions a new goal.

OCTOBER 2, 2022

Plan →
- Funnel to the center of body.
- Extend glove hand slightly more.

Implement →
- Work on funneling during dailies.
- Funnel center of body every rep.
- In dailies, find comfort for better glove extension.

Scoring →
- Funnel center of body. → 2.7
- Better glove extension. → 2.6

Review →
- I am beginning to notice at times, I don't funnel center-cut. I still need more work on mastering this, which is where dailies can help.
- I have found a comfortable glove extension to help me get the short hop. I can still be better at getting my glove out there on forehand plays.

Figure 5.9: Week two player two reflection two.

Wow! The specificity regarding player two's reflection is impressive. He even added a new goal, embedding the *what* by addressing which parts of practice drills were applicable to focus on his new goal (funneling during *dailies*—the daily work drills the infielders do each day). Notice also that in his review, player two identified he needed to work on mastering funneling center of body (or center-cut). This was a perfect example of a player seeing the direct connection between essential skills, developmental sports scales, and practice drills! Player two also recognized the parts of practice important to this new goal were different and provided a specific, repeatable situation for practiced success. This was a great progression in understanding the components of each goal and how they differed in the approach taken. Player two rated his goal success at 2.7. There was improvement, but not complete proficiency.

Figure 5.10 shows Coach Heflebower's feedback to player two's week two reflection.

> **LOVE THE REFLECTION OF NOTICING GREAT PLAYS BEING EASY WHEN YOUR FUNDAMENTALS ARE IN ORDER.**
>
> YOU CAN NOW USE THIS TO CHALLENGE YOURSELF BECAUSE IF YOUR FUNDAMENTALS ARE MAKING YOU BETTER-ON GREAT PLAYS-YOU CAN PUSH YOUR RANGE EVEN FARTHER. WHAT PARTS OF THE SIX FS ARE GOING TO BE KEY FOR THIS CONTINUED GROWTH?

Figure 5.10: Week two coach feedback two.

This is the ultimate goal—to see the player self-assess and learn where successes and failures come in the process of reflection and detailed goal work. Player two's second review was detailed and talked about the building blocks starting to come together to see productive and successful end results in large-scale goals. Again, it is worth noting Coach Heflebower practiced quality feedback tactics. Even in a stronger player reflection, there was still room for his question to increase player thinking and agency.

During the third week reflection, player two's initial goal was well put together, with process *and* result-specific details. Note because Coach Heflebower was specific, player two's reflective statements were also specific. This player also understood how to describe the *feel* for something, which is often a challenging concept for a coach to describe. Figure 5.11 shows player two's third-week reflection.

OCTOBER 9, 2022

Plan →	– Work on a better first step.
	– Use smoother backhand transfers.
Implement →	– Stick to daily work, but emphasize good backhand work.
	– During batting practice, always work on having a good pre-pitch and first step, then each pitch and rep.
Scoring →	– First step = 2.7
	– Backhands = 2.5
Review →	– Taking notice of having a better first step has made me realize it's importance to make great plays look easy. I can keep working in practice to master it.
	– The six Fs drill will make my feet work better in sync for backhand plays.

Figure 5.11: Week three player two reflection.

Verbalizing the goal successfully led to excellent self-coaching—player two knew if something was unsuccessful, what it should *feel* like when corrected, and how to adjust to get back on track. Player two rated goal success at 2.7.

Coach Heflebower provided his week three feedback during an in-person meeting. During that time, he discussed the importance of understanding how to put into words what the player was feeling. This not only served the player in the moment but also supported him to use personal cues to make adjustments on the fly instead of after the fact.

Player two is an exceptionally gifted athlete in the physical realm; his mental capability to identify the necessary adjustments and verbalize them served him well. He made greater gains than player one. Player two saw more success in his development because of his greater detail—putting into words what his goals were, how they were going to work for him, and why they were important for success.

DISCUSSION

Although both players improved during the three-week process, player two's ability to use the language from the developmental sports scale (while articulating his goals and strategies) allowed for more overall improvement. The improvement was more noticeable in the coach's observations because player two excelled where player one did not. Player two's ability to verbalize his goals and articulate the process to reach those goals helped the coach better understand and communicate instruction on a deeper level than when he did with player one. Both players are extremely talented and would rank overall in the higher end of the developmental sports scales for infielders in glove work and footwork. However, player one lacked the ability to externally process and verbalize his journey in development, whereas player two clearly understood that by feeling and describing details, he could make adjustments more rapidly and, therefore, achieve more expeditious success.

Baseball, like many other sports, is an instant-results game—success and failure in every aspect of the game are immediate and individualized. Proper fundamentals and execution of the fundamentals provide a successfully completed task the players see come to fruition right away. Players who struggle to self-assess on the fly but understand the cues they or their coaches have established for success will see both positive and negative play results. However, these players may not see the *what*, *how*, and *why* of the process that led them to those results. This case study provided coaches with a baseline assessment plan and coaching approach for player self-reflection. This way, all game results can be understood, felt, and adjusted after reviewing the event. Coaches then proceeded with a new plan to implement a detail or cue to set the player back on the right track for success in a specific aspect of the game.

Although this case study occurred at the collegiate level, the understanding is generalized. Players who know specific expectations, take time to reflect, and receive specific, criteria-related, and timely feedback from their coaches significantly improve.

High School Experiential Vignette

At the high school level, Coach Heflebower learned the importance of communication among all parties (coaches, players, and parents) and the integral role developmental sports scales play in helping remove the personal side of coaching judgments. Using the essential skills allowed the coach to provide more thoughtful and objective judgments.

Coach Heflebower completed this reflection during the 2021–2022 school year while he was in the position of head baseball coach in a smaller-sized high school located in a Western state. As the new head coach, he recognized early on there were a few significant player types that made up this program. Previously, the program had little structure; there was ample chaos, drama, rumors, entitlement, and other concerning behaviors from both players and parents. They all had opinions about who they were, how good they were, how good other players were, and so on. Coach Heflebower knew he needed to establish concrete expectations everyone would understand. He needed to determine the standards for the program and the direction it would be headed.

The following accounts describe how Coach Heflebower used the developmental sports scales with two different players. As any coach knows, teams are made of diverse personalities with different levels of work ethic, motivations, and skill sets. The developmental sports scales provided a concrete basis for objective reasoning, and the coach could easily communicate this to players and parents to avert questions or concerns.

During the first mandatory player and parent meeting, Coach Heflebower and his coaching team collectively laid out the program expectations, rules, and policies. The coach then articulated how he would use developmental sports scales to separate the seemingly subjective coaching judgments from the more objective ones. He hoped this would curtail the gossip, rumors, playing time complaints, or cries of unfair treatment that had previously plagued the baseball program.

BACKGROUND

The two players discussed in this section were vastly different in their effort and skill sets, yet vying for the same starting position. Player one was a senior and previous two-year starting infielder. At first glance, he had notable credentials to contend for another starting position that upcoming season. Player two was a freshman with very raw physical talent who demonstrated strong potential early on. Coach Heflebower and his coaching team used the following two developmental sports scales to work with the players. Figure 5.12 (page 108) shows essential skills needed for positioning and making plays.

First, the coaching team worked together to calibrate their understanding to ensure they shared consistent expectations. Next, they used the scales during tryouts for objectively identifying and scoring the players.

Figure 5.13 (page 109) shows the second developmental sports scale, which specifically referenced the perceived elusive, yet important skills encompassing expectations for participation and learning.

Area: Infielding

Topic: Positioning and Making Plays

			Observations
3.0		**In addition to 2.0 knowledge and skills, the player demonstrates deeper applications and fluency with skills.** For example: • Adapts easily to various surfaces (dirt or turf) in positioning • Adjusts infield positioning based on player knowledge of batting team player tendencies • Leads and communicates pickoff plays with other infielders	
	2.5	Player exhibits all the score 2.0 components and some of the elite 3.0 components.	
2.0		**Expected player proficiencies** • Awareness of opposing base runners • Knowledge of other infielder tendencies in positioning and who plays which balls • Adjusts positioning based on coach direction • Confidence in picking skills • Comfort working in concert with catcher to position pickoff plays • Correct foot-to-bag positioning for various runners **The player exhibits no major errors or omissions.**	
	1.5	Player exhibits all the score 1.0 components and some of the 2.0 components.	

1.0		**Player knows and demonstrates basic knowledge and skills:**
		
		• Recognizes or recalls specific sport terminology, such as—
		  → *foot to bag*
		  → *pickoff plays*
		  → *base runners*
		
		Simpler knowledge and skills:
		
		• Demonstrates limited awareness of opposing base runners; often hesitates before throwing
		• Uncertain of other teammate infielder tendencies in positioning and who plays which balls; hesitation or collisions when playing balls up the middle
		• Uncertain of where to position based on batters, even with coach direction
		• Picks off base runners only occasionally
		• Demonstrates catcher and infielder confusion on pickoff plays
		• Positions feet on bag incorrectly	

Figure 5.12: Developmental sports scale for positioning and making plays.

Topic: Expectations for Participation and Learning			
Level: High School			
3.0	**In addition to 2.0 knowledge and skills, the player demonstrates deeper applications and fluency with skills.** For example: • Demonstrates team leadership and involvement exceeding expectations, such as organizing the team for practice, actively assisting other players to help them understand, and so on • Focuses on the task exceeding expectations, such as being self-directed and having an enthusiastic attitude • Prepares to learn exceeding expectations by arriving early to practice and consistently working hard • Exceeds deadlines and practice expectations by turning in reflections with honest and detailed information and holding self to a high standard		Observations
	2.5	Player exhibits all the score 2.0 components and some of the elite 3.0 components.	
2.0	**Expected player proficiencies** • Leads and is actively involved in practice situations and discussions by sharing information and sometimes even performing a leadership role • Focuses on the practice task by working independently, self-adjusting, and exhibiting a positive attitude • Prepares to learn by being on time, bringing proper equipment, and showing up ready to work hard • Meets deadlines and practice expectations		
	1.5	Player exhibits all the score 1.0 components and some of the 2.0 components.	

1.0	**Player knows and demonstrates basic knowledge and skills:**
	
	• Recognizes or recalls specific sport terminology, such as—
	    → *leads during practice*
	    → *shows a positive attitude*
	    → *practice expectations*
	Simpler knowledge and skills:
	
	• Demonstrates reduced involvement in practice situations; requires prompts to participate, relies on the contributions of others, and struggles to initiate sharing information
	• Attends practice inconsistently; struggles to arrive on time, bring proper equipment, and be ready to work hard
	• Focuses on the task only with frequent reminders and relies on others to perform the drill or model techniques
	• Prepared to learn only with frequent reminders to be on time, bring equipment, and be ready to practice
	• Struggles to meet practice quality expectations, needing consistent reminders to review a skill and modify form
	• Demonstrates awareness of deadlines and practice quality expectations inconsistently; initiates arrangements with coach to address lateness or redo skills		

Figure 5.13: Developmental sports scale for expectations for participation and learning.

The coaches used this scale to address the universal skills of each player's abilities to participate, adhere to expectations, and learn.

SCENARIO FOR PLAYER ONE

Player one arrived late to the first day of tryouts and did not attend any optional early fall workouts prior to the season. During the first tryout, player one scored in the 1.0–1.5 range for both positioning and making plays; additionally, he scored at the same level in expectations for participation and learning—both below the expected proficient level, indicating a lack in the basic fundamentals and player behaviors needed to be a successful infielder at the high school level. Player one demonstrated a sense of entitlement from his previous success, saying, "Well . . . I started varsity last year." As he vocalized that comment (among others), the coach wondered if the new expectations for *demonstrating* skills (not simply professing them) would challenge player one.

As the season progressed, the developmental sports scales proved invaluable. Five games into the season, Coach Heflebower clearly communicated the reasons player one was not having the success he (and his parents) thought he deserved. As Coach Heflebower used the developmental sports scales as an objective tool to articulate the expectations. Player one understood his lack of playing time was directly connected to *his* lack of effort toward growth on both the physical and intangible components needed to be proficient in the game. Player one eventually quit the team.

As we mentioned in chapter 2 (page 43), integrity is essential. When you (as the coach) clearly articulate your expectations, paired with what you will and won't accept in the program, players not only see what they must do but also must decide if they are willing to accept and abide by your articulated parameters. Although having a player quit is not the hope or goal of any program, this action helped keep such decisions from becoming as personal as they might have been otherwise. Using the developmental sports scales that highlighted Coach Heflebower's expectations for players in his program helped his entire team see he would act with integrity—doing what he said he would do. The team regrouped and collectively became more cohesive. This was an interesting by-product of an otherwise difficult situation.

SCENARIO FOR PLAYER TWO

Player two, a freshman, also fell into the 1.0–1.5 score range on the first scale (positioning and making plays), which addressed the fundamental skills for infielding. However, player two was much better when assessed on the second scale addressing expectations for participation and learning. His participation and learning were consistently at the 2.0–2.5 levels. Player two was one of the hardest workers on the team. He bought into the program expectations right away and appreciated the clarity and transparency. Additionally, he quickly gained respect for the coaching team members when they stood behind their decisions to review players fairly and objectively. These two scales helped player two tremendously in understanding exactly what the coaching team expected of him for success, and the scales helped him grow and mature under Coach Heflebower's guidance regarding the physical and fundamental skills required to be proficient in the game. Player two garnered the starting infield position and ended the season with enough votes from opposing coaches in the conference to be named a first team all-conference player!

Developmental sports scales help coaches clearly identify what is important and share that information with players. Although using scales didn't curtail the difficult decision or situation with player one described in this section, it did prove beneficial in communicating the skills and behaviors the coach expected of all players. Player two not only improved immensely but also became a respected leader among other coaches in the conference.

REFLECTIONS

Reflecting on these two situations, we speculate there was something more that propelled player two over player one for the starting role and overall season success. However, the facts remain that using the same developmental sports scales helped Coach Heflebower and his coaching team differentiate between two players to help maintain the team's established expectations and standards. It is important to note coaches using scales may choose to weigh the intangibles scale (expectations for participation and learning) heavier than the fundamental skills scale (positioning and making plays). That was true in this case—Coach Heflebower placed more emphasis on the intangibles scale. He felt he could teach the baseball fundamentals to a player willing to participate and learn, as opposed to trying to change the attitude of a player who behaved as though he was entitled to the position. Instruction about position fundamentals is much easier and more successful when the players' participation levels and learning are on the right track. So if a coach is going to place the weight on these scales differently, like Coach Heflebower did, it is paramount the coach communicate that difference from the very start. Failure to communicate this to players (and parents) could lead to discrepancies that complicate the scale-based judgments after the fact.

It is vital when implementing developmental sports scales at the high school level to share them far enough in advance so no players are uncertain about expectations. When athletes play multiple sports, they often have overlapping seasons. Plan ahead to gather all players for the upcoming season at the same time. Your coaching team needs to carefully plan, calibrate, and communicate. Be certain to plan how the coaching team will establish and uphold each scale. Integrate the scales into preseason discussions with your coaching team as well as daily practices, tryouts, and feedback loops with players. Some coaches even use video examples from players of previous years to establish *reliability* among the coaching team. This simply means each coach understands each of the developmental sports scales and uses them to first independently denote strengths and weaknesses of players shared on video. Afterward, coaches discuss their independent observations and ratings with one another. They detail their discussions to better establish their reliability. When using developmental sports scales, it shouldn't matter which coach is observing players—the expectations and judgments should be consistent. More detail about this process can be found in *Leading Standards-Based Learning: An Implementation Guide for Schools and Districts* (Heflebower et al., 2021, pp. 81–83).

Using developmental sports scales increases player intrinsic motivation. As you read in chapter 2 (page 28), when players have increased autonomy in developing their competencies, their intrinsic motivation increases. This competency occurs when players use scales for understanding expectations for success, self-assessment, reflection, and goal setting, paired with quality feedback from coaches. These practices help high school athletes develop both in the sport-specific skills *and* behaviors. While instruction can be messy at times, players should never feel as if expectations are a mystery. Clear and consistent communication from the coaches to the players breeds a set of program expectations foundational to player growth and team success. Coach Heflebower culled these findings and reflections into a final summary in the following succinct list.

- **Establish and clearly communicate expectations:** Be sure the players know how you will evaluate them.

- **Adjust scales and expectations as needed:** Be sure scales and expectations are set to reflect realistic goals for the specific team—too high or low can be detrimental. Slide the scale up or down as needed (see chapter 3, page 65).

- **Encourage and challenge:** Help players internalize your guidance on the expectations so they understand what you expect of them and perform accordingly. Encourage players when needed, and challenge them as warranted. Use the scales to differentiate your coaching to the individual needs of your players.

Summary

In this chapter, you witnessed how Coach Heflebower used this book's methods in two different coaching situations. During the collegiate case study, you read about how and when he used the scales with his athletes during practice, collected reflections, and shared feedback. Using the strategies discussed up to this point proved poignant in improving athletic performance. In the detailed high school vignette, you witnessed how using scales with different athletes enabled the coach to glean objective evaluations from players. Finally, you accessed the lessons Coach Heflebower learned, as well as his suggestions for embedding developmental sports scales into your practice.

Epilogue

Organized sports run the gamut and are amazing in many ways. They provide an arena in which student athletes can grow their physical and emotional capacity, learn key life lessons, find inspiration, gain experience working with peers, and develop relationships with coaches. They also provide unique opportunities for coaches to hone their craft, nurture players' abilities, and collaborate with parents. Despite the many rewards of their position, coaches encounter unique challenges.

Coaches work with increasingly diverse populations and face heightening demands from their athletes, their athletes' parents and caregivers, administrators, and fans. Coaches are required to fulfill a variety of roles that may include educator, guide, sports psychologist, and business manager. Additionally, young athletes' needs are evolving. In the world of school sports, there is a new emphasis on positive interaction and the overall development of athletes rather than simply the win-loss record. There is greater accessibility to information and visibility to a larger community in the digital age. All these factors make coaching both more exciting and more taxing than ever before. Because of this immense responsibility, coaches can and should improve and expand their capabilities to meet the needs of the athletes they serve.

Additionally, schools and other entities that employ coaches are obliged to provide them with sufficient training, philosophical understanding, and practical resources to guide them in their immeasurable roles. This is important not just for coaches but also for parents, caregivers, and families, who make a sizable investment when encouraging a child to participate in school sports. Families make a significant investment of resources for each child involved in youth sports in the form of considerable expenses, time, availability for family and social functions, and physical and emotional health. Parents expend a great deal of time and financial resources for their child to participate in organized school or club sporting activities.

This book's aim was to provide the foundational information and tools coaches need to address these challenges. Chapter 1 (page 11) explored the coaching role, the ten characteristics required for success in the role, and a coaching cycle we've found to be effective for developing those characteristics. Chapter 2 (page 27) demonstrated the importance of fostering a positive player-coach relationship, outlined research about players' development needs, and provided guidance for nurturing authentic relationships with a focus on meeting those needs. Chapter 3 (page 51) established expectations for proficiency-based coaching by illustrating how coaches identify priority knowledge and skills athletes need to thrive in their sport and use developmental sports scales to communicate those expectations to athletes. Chapter 4 (page 75) illustrated how to use developmental sports scales for tracking progress, providing players with meaningful feedback, and helping them set achievable goals for their growth. Finally, chapter 5 (page 97) provided a case study of Coach Heflebower's experience using developmental sports scales with athletes at both the college and high school levels so you could see how this book's guidance and tools work in a real-life context.

Because of its comprehensive approach, this book is an excellent tool for coaches at all stages of their career—whether they're first grabbing the whistle or getting ready to hang it up! We hope you found the guidance useful and will use it to challenge yourself to be even better.

Generic Developmental Sports Scale Template

Coaches can use developmental sports scales for all types of sports to communicate and assess essential knowledge, skills, and intangibles. The reproducible "Sample Developmental Sports Scale Template" provides a generic developmental sports scale template you can customize for your particular sport and team. Based on the level of your athletes, the amount of time you have players in your sport, and level of play, you may adjust this developmental sports scale to meet your specific needs.

Sample Developmental Sports Scale Template

Sport:		
Area:		
Topic or Position:		
Level:		

3.0	**In addition to 2.0 knowledge and skills, the player demonstrates deeper applications and fluency with skills.** For example: • • • • • • • • • •	**Observations**
	2.5 Player exhibits all the score 2.0 components and some of the elite 3.0 components.	
2.0	**Expected player proficiencies** • • • • • • • • • • **The player exhibits no major errors or omissions.**	
	1.5 Player exhibits all the score 1.0 components and some of the 2.0 components.	

1.0	**Player knows and demonstrates basic knowledge and skills:**
	
	• Recognizes or recalls specific sport terminology, such as—
	   →
	   →
	   →
	
	Simpler knowledge and skills:
	
	•
	•
	•
	•
	•	

Developmental Sports Scales for Baseball

Developmental sports scales are a coach's best tools for effectively promoting, coaching, and evaluating knowledge, skills, and intangibles with their athletes. This appendix contains a set of developmental sports scales for baseball. Based on the level of your athletes, the amount of time you have players in your sport, and level of play, you may adjust any of the following developmental sports scales to meet your specific needs.

Sample Prioritized Criteria for Baseball Infielding

→ Glove positioning and ball handling

→ Eyes and ball tracking

→ Footwork and range

Glove Positioning and Ball Handling Developmental Sports Scale Template

Sport: Baseball

Area: Infielding

Topic: Glove Positioning and Ball Handling

3.0	In addition to 2.0 knowledge and skills, the player demonstrates deeper applications and fluency with skills. For example: • Adapts easily to various surfaces (dirt or turf) when placing glove and anticipating ball hops • Adjusts to weather and other field conditions for glove placement and ball tracking	Observations
	2.5 Player exhibits all the score 2.0 components and some of the elite 3.0 components.	
2.0	**Expected player proficiencies** • Early glove presentation • Relaxed glove presentation • No wasted movement of glove • Glove leads player to the ball • Hands out in front • Hands pushed through the hops • Consistent catching and receiving of ball in the same spot in glove • Funnels the ball to center of chest **The player exhibits no major errors or omissions.**	
	1.5 Player exhibits all the score 1.0 components and some of the 2.0 components.	

1.0	**Player knows and demonstrates basic knowledge and skills:**
	• Recognizes or recalls specific sport terminology, such as—
	  → *glove presentation*
	  → *hands pushed through the hops*
	  → *funnels*
	Simpler knowledge and skills:
	• Late glove presentation
	• Tense glove presentation
	• Wasted movement of glove (glove shaking, twisting, and so on)
	• Glove doesn't consistently lead player to the ball
	• Hands not out front in ready position
	• Hands not pushed through the hops
	• Inconsistent catching and receiving of ball in the same spot in glove
	• Inconsistently funnels the ball to center of chest	

Eyes and Ball Tracking Developmental Sports Scale Template

Developmental Sports Scales for Baseball

			Observations
Sport: Baseball			
Area: Infielding			
Topic: Eyes and Ball Tracking			
3.0	**In addition to score 2.0, the player demonstrates deeper applications and fluency with skills.** For example: • Adapts easily to various surfaces (dirt or turf) when tracking the ball • Adjusts to weather and other field conditions for eye movement and ball tracking		
	2.5	Player exhibits all the score 2.0 components and some of the elite 3.0 components.	
2.0	**Expected player proficiencies** • Eyes low in line with the ball • Eyes behind the ball when backing up • Seeing the ball hit the glove • Keeping head steady on the ball hops • Trusting hands so eyes are on correct approach • Identifies the ground ball style quickly and accurately **The player exhibits no major errors or omissions.**		
	1.5	Player exhibits all the score 1.0 components and some of the 2.0 components.	

1.0	**Player knows and demonstrates basic knowledge and skills:**
	
	• Recognizes or recalls specific sport terminology, such as:
	  → *eyes in line*
	  → *trusting hands*
	  → *ground ball style*
	
	Simpler knowledge and skills:
	
	• Eyes too high, and not in line with the ball
	• Eyes looking incorrectly at the ball when backing up
	• Not seeing the ball hit the glove
	• Head unsteady on the ball hops
	• Not trusting hands so eyes are on correct approach
	• Inaccurately or too slowly identifying the ground ball style		

Footwork and Range Developmental Sports Scale Template

Sport: Baseball		
Area: Infielding		
Topic: Footwork and Range		
3.0	In addition to score 2.0, the player demonstrates deeper applications and fluency with skills. For example: • Adapts footwork easily to various surfaces (dirt or turf) • Adjusts to weather and other field conditions for range	**Observations**
	2.5 Player exhibits all the score 2.0 components and some of the elite 3.0 components.	
2.0	**Expected player proficiencies** • Quick and efficient first step • Movement directly to the baseball (no wasted steps) • Sets feet up to field in position to throw immediately after • Smooth flow—not choppy or stuttered • Correct angles cut to the ball based on the type of ground ball • Feet move to create good hops (move in or back to catch off ground or in air) • Follows the throw **The player exhibits no major errors or omissions.**	
	1.5 Player exhibits all the score 1.0 components and some of the 2.0 components.	
1.0	**Player knows and demonstrates basic knowledge and skills:** • Recognizes or recalls specific sport terminology, such as— → *stuttered* → *correct angle* → *good hops* **Simpler knowledge and skills:** • Slow first step • Wasted steps to the baseball • Feet out of position to throw immediately after fielding • Stuttered steps • Angles inaccurate to the ball when fielding • Feet out of position to move or catch ball off ground or in air • Doesn't follow the throw	

Developmental Sports Scales for Basketball

This appendix contains a set of developmental sports scales for basketball. Based on the level of your athletes, the amount of time you have players in your sport, and level of play, you may adjust any of the following developmental sports scales to meet your specific needs.

Sample Prioritized Criteria for Basketball

→ Defense

→ Ball handling

→ Shooting

Defense Developmental Sports Scale Template

Sport: Basketball			
Topic: Defense			
Level: High School			
3.0	**In addition to 2.0 knowledge and skills, the player demonstrates deeper applications and fluency with skills.** For example: • Reads offensive plays and easily adjusts defense (2–1–2, 1-3-1, person–person) • Anticipates offensive passes and shots to steal the ball		**Observations**
	2.5	Player exhibits all the score 2.0 components and some of the elite 3.0 components.	
2.0	**Expected player proficiencies** • Laterally moves with the player defending • Anticipates the pass or dribble directional change • Fronts player when cutting • Sees both the ball and the player • Moves to unguarded player with the ball **The player exhibits no major errors or omissions.**		
	1.5	Player exhibits all the score 1.0 components and some of the 2.0 components.	

1.0	**Player knows and demonstrates basic knowledge and skills:**
	• Recognizes or recalls specific sport terminology, such as—
	   → *offside*
	   → *help defense*
	   → *lateral movement*
	   → *anticipation and fronting*
	Simpler knowledge and skills:
	• Slow and cumbersome lateral movement
	• Limited, if any, anticipation of offensive player moves to pass or change directions while dribbling
	• Follows offensive player on cuts
	• Loses player with the ball
	• Refrains from helping out on offside defense		

Ball Handling Developmental Sports Scale Template

Sport: Basketball

Topic: Ball Handling

Level: High School

			Observations
3.0		**In addition to 2.0 knowledge and skills, the player demonstrates deeper applications and fluency with skills.** For example: • Uses behind-the-back or between-the-legs maneuvers to switch hands and divert the defense while dribbling • Maintains control of the ball even when under pressing defense—knows when to dribble and pass • Confidently moves through the lane even with intensive defensive pressure	
	2.5	Player exhibits all the score 2.0 components and some of the elite 3.0 components.	
2.0		**Expected player proficiencies** • Handles ball evenly with both hands • Keeps eyes up looking down court, not at the ball • Moves quickly with the ball • Transitions easily to passing and shooting • Drives to the basket fluidly, even on defense **The player exhibits no major errors or omissions.**	
	1.5	Player exhibits all the score 1.0 components and some of the 2.0 components.	
1.0		**Player knows and demonstrates basic knowledge and skills:** • Recognizes or recalls specific sport terminology, such as— → *transitioning from dribbling* → *offensive ability* → *driving to basket* → *ball handling* **Simpler knowledge and skills:** • Difficulty dribbling with nondominant hand • Eyes are not always looking up court—often at ball or back and forth • Slow when dribbling and running at the same time • Difficulty transitioning from dribbling to passing or shooting • Limited offensive dribbling ability	

Coaching Competitive Sports © 2024 Marzano Resources • MarzanoResources.com
Visit **MarzanoResources.com/reproducibles** to download this free reproducible.

Shooting Developmental Sports Scale Template

Sport: Basketball
Topic: Shooting
Level: High School

			Observations
3.0		**In addition to 2.0 knowledge and skills, the player demonstrates deeper applications and fluency with skills.**	
		For example:	
		• Successfully aligns upper body, arm, and hands, even when lower body is off-balance	
		• Modifies shooting technique and touch for different situations—fingertip rolls, dunks, and three-point shots	
	2.5	Player exhibits all the score 2.0 components and some of the elite 3.0 components.	
2.0		**Expected player proficiencies**	
		• Body squared to the basket	
		• Shooting elbow at ninety degrees	
		• Legs engaged for added power	
		• Follow-through; ball rotation has backspin and the hand flips downward with index finger pointing toward basket	
		• Fluid movement from pass or dribble to shooting position through follow-through	
		• Knowing when to shoot (open) or pass to a teammate	
		The player exhibits no major errors or omissions.	
	1.5	Player exhibits all the score 1.0 components and some of the 2.0 components.	
1.0		**Player knows and demonstrates basic knowledge and skills:**	
		• Recognizes or recalls specific sport terminology, such as—	
		→ *squared to basket*	
		→ *arm at ninety*	
		Simpler knowledge and skills:	
		• Body not squared to the basket	
		• Elbow of shooting arm sticks out at forty-five degree angle	
		• Relies on arm power rather than bending knees, thus limiting distance power	
		• Lacks follow-through; hand pops back and doesn't bend toward basket or point the index finger	
		• Limited or lack of fluidity transitioning from dribble or pass to shooting position	
		• Takes shots when not open rather than passing to a teammate	

Developmental Sports Scales for Football

This appendix contains a set of football developmental sports scales specifically for the football positions of safety, punter, and quarterback. Based on additional positions, the level of your athletes, the amount of time you have players in your sport, and level of play, you may adjust any of the following developmental sports scales to meet your specific needs.

Sample Prioritized Criteria for Football Key Positions

→ Safety

→ Punter

→ Quarterback

Safety Developmental Sports Scale Template

Sport: Football
Position: Safety
Level: High School

			Observations
3.0		**In addition to 2.0 knowledge and skills, the player demonstrates deeper applications and fluency with skills.** For example: • Reads the ball well and knows when to move in front of the receiver for interceptions • Regularly makes effective tackles to prevent opposing team from scoring	
	2.5	Player exhibits all the score 2.0 components and some of the elite 3.0 components.	
2.0		**Expected player proficiencies** • Reads multiple cues correctly for run or pass • Follows ball—covers receivers • Closes ground to receiver when ball is in the air • Makes solid tackles in open field • Makes a play on the ball for interceptions • Doesn't allow any opposing player to be deeper than him **The player exhibits no major errors or omissions.**	
	1.5	Player exhibits all the score 1.0 components and some of the 2.0 components.	

1.0		**Player knows and demonstrates basic knowledge and skills:**
		• Recognizes or recalls specific sport terminology, such as—
		  → *multiple cues*
		  → *solid tackles*
		  → *play on the ball*
		Simpler knowledge and skills:
		• Fails to recognize cues for the run or pass
		• Has difficulty following the ball and knowing which receivers to cover
		• Moves too slowly to close ground on receiver
		• Fails to contact and wrap up offensive player resulting in weak tackles
		• Hands are stiff or bobbles interception opportunities
		• Allows receivers to get more toward endzone	

Punter Developmental Sports Scale Template

Sport: Football		
Position: Punter		
Level: High School		

			Observations
3.0		**In addition to 2.0 knowledge and skills, the player demonstrates deeper applications and fluency with skills.** For example: • Reception of ball effortless—easily spins laces to the top every time • Footwork quick and agile in difficult situations (weather, defenders approaching, snap is off) • Ball drop consistent in the same place every time • Flexibility and extension of leg and follow-through correct height and extended to the maximum • Leg strength powerful, bringing entire body off the ground after contact for maximum distance	
	2.5	Player exhibits all the score 2.0 components and some of the elite 3.0 components.	
2.0		**Expected player proficiencies** • Clean reception of the snap • Feet properly aligned, purposeful steps to contact • Drop of ball consistent • Leg follow-through after contact extended, pointing toward target • Strong leg for power and distance **The player exhibits no major errors or omissions.**	
	1.5	Player exhibits all the score 1.0 components and some of the 2.0 components.	

1.0		**Player knows and demonstrates basic knowledge and skills:**
		
		• Recognizes or recalls specific sport terminology, such as—
		   → *clean reception*
		   → *drop of ball*
		Simpler knowledge and skills:
		
		• Inconsistent hands when receiving the ball from center—bobbles or drops occur
		• Steps to contact slow and staggered due to incorrect line up
		• Drop of ball inconsistent and off
		• Limited follow-through with leg toward target
		• Weak leg strength for limited punting distance	

Quarterback Developmental Sports Scale Template

Sport: Football			
Position: Quarterback			
Level: High School			
3.0	**In addition to 2.0 knowledge and skills, the player demonstrates deeper applications and fluency with skills.** For example: • Accurately throws to receivers even under intense coverage and pressure • Leads receivers in ways to mitigate interceptions • Easily modifies plays at the line of scrimmage based on defensive positions of opposing team		**Observations**
	2.5	Player exhibits all the score 2.0 components and some of the elite 3.0 components.	
2.0	**Expected player proficiencies** • Receives ball well from center, either direct snap or shotgun • Gets the ball up in passing ready position • Throws accurately to target • Makes correct number of drop steps for the play call • Reads defense positions accurately to adjust play **The player exhibits no major errors or omissions.**		
	1.5	Player exhibits all the score 1.0 components and some of the 2.0 components.	

1.0	**Player knows and demonstrates basic knowledge and skills:**
	• Recognizes or recalls specific sport terminology, such as—
	  → *snap*
	  → *shotgun*
	  → *drop steps*
	  → *ready passing position*
	  → *defense positions*
	  → *pocket*
	Simpler knowledge and skills:
	• Difficulty receiving snap from center or shotgun, bobbles or drops ball often
	• Fails to get ball up into the ready passing position
	• Limited accuracy in throwing to target
	• Incorrect drop steps in the pocket
	• Unable to see defenders correctly to adjust play		

Developmental Sports Scales for Softball

This appendix contains developmental sports scales for pitching in softball. Based on the level of your athletes, the amount of time you have players in your sport, and level of play, you may adjust any of the following developmental sports scales to meet your specific needs. Note that the pitch counts will vary based on age.

Sample Prioritized Criteria for Softball Pitching

- → Accuracy
- → Velocity and spin
- → Execution

Pitching Accuracy Developmental Sports Scale Template

Sport: Softball			
Topic: Pitching Accuracy			
Level: High School			
3.0	**In addition to 2.0 knowledge and skills, the player demonstrates deeper applications and fluency with skills.** For example: • Maintains endurance and consistency of pitches through seven or more game-like innings • Uses strategy and awareness of effective pitch combinations for various players without much coaching direction • Changes pitch location based on count; for example, when an athlete's count is 0–2, player can throw an off-speed pitch slightly outside the strike zone		**Observations**
	2.5	Player exhibits all the score 2.0 components and some of the elite 3.0 components.	
2.0	**Expected player proficiencies** • Throws an outside pitch (curveball, drop ball, and so on) with 80 percent accuracy • Throws an inside pitch (screwball, rise ball, and so on) with 80 percent accuracy • Throws an off-speed pitch (changeup, off-speed, and so on) with 80 percent accuracy • Adjusts inside and outside pitches in the location of the strike zone with 50 percent accuracy **The player exhibits no major errors or omissions.**		
	1.5	Player exhibits all the score 1.0 components and some of the 2.0 components.	

1.0	**Player knows and demonstrates basic knowledge and skills:**
	• Recognizes or recalls specific sport knowledge, such as—
	  → *Terms for different pitches*
	  → *An understanding of pitches and where they should be thrown*
	• How to throw different pitches
	Simpler knowledge and skills:
	• Can consistently throw strikes
	• Is safely developing spin pitches, such as the screwball, curveball, or rise ball		

Developmental Sports Scales for Softball

Pitching Velocity and Spin Developmental Sports Scale Template

Sport: Softball			
Topic: Pitching Velocity and Spin			
Level: High School			
3.0	**In addition to 2.0 knowledge and skills, the player demonstrates deeper applications and fluency with skills.** For example: • Maintains stamina through seven innings while keeping momentum and arm speed to keep pitches at top speed • Maintains stamina through seven innings while keeping spin and movement on every pitch • Attacks the count with confidence, consistently putting spin and speed on every pitch		**Observations**
	2.5	Player exhibits all the score 2.0 components and some of the elite 3.0 components.	
2.0	**Expected player proficiencies** • Accelerates arm speed throughout the motion, ending at player's top speed • Uses front foot to push momentum forward • Moves through the pitch; that is, momentum continues forward after the pitch • Actively engages forearm and wrist to create spin and movement on the ball • Keeps hips clear and perpendicular to home plate to leave space for arm and wrist		
	1.5	Player exhibits all the score 1.0 components and some of the 2.0 components.	

1.0	**Player knows and demonstrates basic knowledge and skills:**
	
	• Recognizes or recalls specific sport terminology, such as—
	  → *accelerating arm speed*
	  → *holding body in a stacked position*
	
	Simpler knowledge and skills:
	
	• Safely uses wrist and forearm to add some spin
	• Holds body in a stacked position
	• Accelerates throughout motion		

Coaching Competitive Sports © 2024 Marzano Resources • MarzanoResources.com
Visit **MarzanoResources.com/reproducibles** to download this free reproducible.

Developmental Sports Scales for Softball

Pitching Execution Developmental Sports Scale Template

Sport: Softball

Topic: Pitching Execution

Level: High School

3.0	In addition to 2.0 knowledge and skills, the player demonstrates deeper applications and fluency with skills.		**Observations**
	For example: <ul><li>Leads others defensively; has situational awareness and communicates to teammates what the next play should be</li><li>Cleanly and consistently fields ground balls and pop flies, and defends bunts with very few errors in a season</li><li>Starts ahead in most counts and throws favorable pitches in a way that allows player to control the count and the game</li><li>Leads with both verbal and nonverbal cues that encourage other players to stay aggressive and confident throughout difficult game situations</li></ul>		
	2.5	Player exhibits all the score 2.0 components and some of the elite 3.0 components.	
2.0	**Expected player proficiencies** <ul><li>Maintains a calm and encouraging demeanor</li><li>Attacks the count and is aggressive when facing a batter</li><li>Cleanly fields ground balls and pop flies, and defends bunts</li><li>Changes the location of the pitch based on the current count</li></ul>		
	1.5	Player exhibits all the score 1.0 components and some of the 2.0 components.	
1.0	**Player knows and demonstrates basic knowledge and skills:** <ul><li>Recognizes or recalls specific sport knowledge, such as—<ul><li>→ *Awareness of situational counts*</li><li>→ *Game awareness, including bunt defenses and monitoring runners*</li></ul></li></ul> **Simpler knowledge and skills:** <ul><li>Stays positive during game-like situations</li><li>Supports teammates</li><li>Completes routine plays in her area</li></ul>		

Developmental Sports Scales for Soccer

This appendix contains a set of developmental sports scales for soccer skills used in many positions that include ball control, passing, spatial awareness, strength and power, and tactical knowledge. Based on the level of your athletes, the amount of time you have players in your sport, and level of play, you may adjust any of the following developmental sports scales to meet your specific needs.

Sample Prioritized Criteria for Soccer

- → Ball control
- → Passing accuracy
- → Spatial awareness
- → Strength and power
- → Tactical knowledge

Ball Control Developmental Sports Scale Template

Sport: Soccer		
Area: Technique		
Topic: Ball Control		
Level: High School		

			Observations
3.0		**In addition to 2.0 knowledge and skills, the player demonstrates deeper applications and fluency with skills.** For example: • Accurately collects the ball under intense pressure and in a tight space • Traps the ball with all parts of body and accurately distributes immediately • Receives and distributes passes with pressure • Understands how to change the pace of the game with one touch versus two touches	
	2.5	Player exhibits all the score 2.0 components and some of the elite 3.0 components.	
2.0		**Expected player proficiencies** • Collects ball and gains control with a close first touch • Traps the ball with head, chest, thigh, and foot • Receives passes on the ground and in the air • Dribbles with head up and with both feet • Maintains possession when turning quickly and with opponent pressure **The student exhibits no major errors or omissions.**	
	1.5	Player exhibits all the score 1.0 components and some of the 2.0 components.	

1.0		**Player knows and demonstrates basic knowledge and skills:**
		• Recognizes or recalls specific sport terminology, such as:
		   → *man on*
		   → *tackle*
		   → *take your space*
		   → *trap*
		Simple knowledge and skills:
		• Collects ball and gains control with a large first touch
		• Traps the ball with thigh and foot
		• Receives passes on the ground
		• Dribbles with head down and one foot
		• Maintains possession without opponent pressure	

Passing Accuracy Developmental Sports Scale Template

Sport: Soccer
Area: Technique
Topic: Passing Accuracy
Level: High School

			Observations
3.0		**In addition to 2.0 knowledge and skills, the player demonstrates deeper applications and fluency with skills.** For example: • Accurately passes using inside of foot, outside of foot, laces, bottom of foot, and so on • Executes a wide range of passes from all distances on the ground and in the air with one touch • Understands when to dribble versus pass and how to draw out defenders	
	2.5	Player exhibits all the score 2.0 components and some of the elite 3.0 components.	
2.0		**Expected player proficiencies** • Uses both feet to pass accurately to other players • Executes passes on the ground and in the air to others • Executes a wide range of passes from short to long distances, whenever the need arises • Accurately passes ball to teammates' desired location to keep play engaged • Knows when to shoot versus pass or cross **The player exhibits no major errors or omissions.**	
	1.5	Player exhibits all the score 1.0 components and some of the 2.0 components.	

1.0		**Player knows and demonstrates basic knowledge and skills:**
		• Recognizes or recalls specific sport terminology, such as—
		  → *cross*
		  → *to feet*
		  → *through ball into space*
		Simpler knowledge and skills:
		• Uses mostly dominant foot to pass somewhat accurately
		• Executes on the ground, but struggles more when ball is in the air
		• Demonstrates range of passes from short to medium distances, but not with precision
		• Attempts passing ball to teammates where desired, but lacks accuracy and consistency
		• Learning to distinguish when to shoot versus pass or cross	

Developmental Sports Scales for Soccer

Spatial Awareness Developmental Sports Scale Template

Sport: Soccer
Area: Game Intelligence
Topic: Spatial Awareness
Level: High School

			Observations
3.0		**In addition to 2.0 knowledge and skills, the player demonstrates deeper applications and fluency with skills.** For example: • Demonstrates awareness of positioning and how to transition when attacking and defending • Knows where surrounding teammates and opponents are to accurately attack and defend • Keeps head up, control of the ball, and mental map of the field	
	2.5	Player exhibits all the score 2.0 components and some of the elite 3.0 components.	
2.0		**Expected player proficiencies** • Awareness of proper positions on the pitch • Knowledge of where self and teammates are at all times • Mindfulness of the surrounding angles and open space • Awareness of opponents' positioning • Instinct to be proactive **The student exhibits no major errors or omissions.**	
	1.5	Player exhibits all the score 1.0 components and some of the 2.0 components.	

1.0		**Player knows and demonstrates basic knowledge and skills:**
		
		• Recognizes or recalls specific sport terminology, such as—
		   → *pitch*
		   → *defender*
		   → *midfielder*
		   → *forward*
		   → *goalkeeper*
		Simpler knowledge and skills:
		
		• Awareness of proper positions on the pitch
		• Knows where self and teammates are only at certain times
		• Relies on coach's cues to be mindful of the surrounding angles and open space
		• Awareness only of the immediate defending opponent
		• Reactive instinct	

Developmental Sports Scales for Soccer

Strength and Power Developmental Sports Scale Template

			Observations
Sport: Soccer			
Area: Physical Fitness			
Topic: Strength and Power			
Level: High School			
3.0	**In addition to score 2.0, the player demonstrates deeper applications and fluency with skills.** For example: • Shields the ball from opponent and distributes appropriately, when in possession and under pressure • Steals the ball from opponent and maintains possession • Shoots and passes with accuracy when fatigued • Wins fifty-fifty balls out of the air and on the ground against opponent, and keeps possession • Maintains the strength to gain possession of the ball in a tackle and distribute the ball accurately		
	2.5	Player exhibits all the score 2.0 components and some of the elite 3.0 components.	
2.0	**Expected player proficiencies** • Shields the ball from opponent when in possession • Steals the ball from opponent • Shoots and passes through fatigue • Wins fifty-fifty balls out of the air against opponent • Maintains the strength to gain possession of the ball in a tackle **The player exhibits no major errors or omissions.**		
	1.5	Player exhibits all the score 1.0 components and some of the 2.0 components.	

1.0	**Player knows and demonstrates basic knowledge and skills:**
	• Recognizes or recalls specific sport terminology, such as—
	  → *shield*
	  → *steal*
	  → *tackle*
	  → *fifty-fifty*
	Simpler knowledge and skills:
	• Keeps the ball exposed to opponent
	• Inability to steal the ball from opponent
	• Ability to shoot and pass before fatigue
	• Wins fifty-fifty balls on the ground against opponent
	• Maintains the strength to attempt to tackle		

Developmental Sports Scales for Soccer

Tactical Knowledge Developmental Sports Scale Template

Sport: Soccer			
Area: Game Intelligence			
Topic: Tactical Knowledge			
Level: High School			
3.0	**In addition to 2.0 knowledge and skills, the player demonstrates deeper applications and fluency with skills.** For example: • Steals the ball, shields the ball from opponents, and accurately completes a pass • Wins fifty-fifty balls out of the air or on the ground and maintains possession • Remains mindful of when to tackle versus when to stay in front of the ball		**Observations**
	2.5	Player exhibits all the score 2.0 components and some of the elite 3.0 components.	
2.0	**The player regularly demonstrates:** • Knowledgeable and adaptable to formation transitions • Familiarity with the advanced rules and structure of the game • Attacks to defending transition moment and vice versa • Prevents the opponent from using angles and open space • Controls the speed of the play **The player exhibits no major errors or omissions.**		
	1.5	Player exhibits all the score 1.0 components and some of the 2.0 components.	

1.0	**Player knows and demonstrates basic knowledge and skills:**
	
	• Recognizes or recalls specific sport terminology, such as—
	   → formations
	   → transitions
	   → speed of play
	
	Simpler knowledge and skills:
	
	• Beginner knowledge of different formations
	• Familiarity with only the basic rules and structure of the game
	• Understands the difference between attacking and defending
	• Defends opponent when attacking
	• Relies on coach's cues to become aware of how to control the speed of play		

Developmental Sports Scales for Track and Field

This appendix contains a set of developmental sports scales for various track and field events including the long jump, shot put, and 400-meter race. Based on the level of your athletes, the amount of time you have players in your sport, and level of play, you may adjust any of the following developmental sports scales to meet your specific needs.

Sample Prioritized Criteria for Track and Field Key Positions

→ Long jump

→ Shot put

→ 400-meter dash

Long Jump Developmental Sports Scale Template

Sport: Track and Field			
Topic: Long Jump			
Level: High School			
3.0		**In addition to 2.0 knowledge and skills, the player demonstrates deeper applications and fluency with skills.** For example: • Sprints maximum speed—faster than average • Adjusts steps flawlessly for changes in conditions (weather, runway surface) • Obtains distances beyond average for level	**Observations**
	2.5	Player exhibits all the score 2.0 components and some of the elite 3.0 components.	
2.0		**Expected player proficiencies** • Sprints to top speed in short distance • Steps are accurate to the board • Maximum height at takeoff from board • Jump load and knee drive present • Stretches and lunges into pit **The player exhibits no major errors or omissions.**	
	1.5	Player exhibits all the score 1.0 components and some of the 2.0 components.	

1.0		**Player knows and demonstrates basic knowledge and skills:**
		
		• Recognizes or recalls specific sport terminology, such as—
		   → *jump load*
		   → *knee drive*
		   → *steps accurate to board*
		   → *stretch and lunge*
		
		Simpler knowledge and skills:
		
		• Speed slows down runway rather than striving for top speed
		• Steps inconsistent, requiring stutter steps toward board
		• Height limited at takeoff
		• Leg drive and jump load not present
		• Lack of stretch and lunge into pit	

Shot Put Developmental Sports Scale Template

Sport: Track and Field		
Topic: Shot Put		
Level: High School		
3.0	**In addition to 2.0 knowledge and skills, the player demonstrates deeper applications and fluency with skills.** For example: • Modifies movement across ring to maximize size and power • Demonstrates maximum explosiveness across ring • Achieves maximum extension on the push for above-average distances	Observations
2.5	Player exhibits all the score 2.0 components and some of the elite 3.0 components.	
2.0	**Expected player proficiencies** • Places put under chin levered into neck • Low, bent starting position • Quick explosiveness across the ring • Low position across ring to maximize leg power • Explodes upward on the turn • Overextension on the push for average distance **The player exhibits no major errors or omissions.**	
1.5	Player exhibits all the score 1.0 components and some of the 2.0 components.	

1.0	**Player knows and demonstrates basic knowledge and skills:**
	
	• Recognizes or recalls specific sport terminology, such as—
	   → *put*
	   → *leverage into chin*
	   → *explosiveness*
	   → *overextension*
	Simpler knowledge and skills:
	
	• Put not clasped under neck and chin
	• Set up high, not leveraging legs
	• Slow across the ring—limited explosiveness
	• Popping up when moving across the ring
	• Slow turn
	• Lack of extension on the push for lower than expected distance	

Developmental Sports Scales for Track and Field

400-Meter Dash Developmental Sports Scale Template

Sport: Track and Field			
Topic: 400-Meter Dash			
Level: High School			
3.0	**In addition to 2.0 knowledge and skills, the player demonstrates deeper applications and fluency with skills.** For example: • Modifies form and function to maximize body type • Alters form and function due to weather or other unforeseen changes in racing conditions • Demonstrates great power and stamina in racing at a consistent pace to obtain better-than-average speed times		**Observations**
	2.5	Player exhibits all the score 2.0 components and some of the elite 3.0 components.	
2.0	**Expected player proficiencies** • Effective and efficient starting position for powerful push off • Long, powerful strides • Arms pushing and pulling with power • Leaning into the curves • Stamina to sustain speed throughout race • Average speed and times for gender and level **The player exhibits no major errors or omissions.**		
	1.5	Player exhibits all the score 1.0 components and some of the 2.0 components.	

1.0	**Player knows and demonstrates basic knowledge and skills:**
	
	• Recognizes or recalls specific sport terminology, such as—
	    → *starting position*
	    → *long and powerful strides*
	    → *stamina*
	    → *leaning into curves*
	Simpler knowledge and skills:
	
	• Ineffective starting position causing slow start
	• Short, choppy strides
	• Arms inefficiently used—hanging or causing inefficient body movements, like arms swinging side to side or tense hands
	• Running the straightaways the same as curves—no leaning or attacking the curves
	• Limited stamina causing speed differences throughout the race (like a quick start)
	• Below-average speed and times for gender and level		

Developmental Sports Scales for Track and Field

Developmental Sports Scales for Volleyball

This appendix contains a set of developmental sports scales for volleyball used in various positions that include attacking from the outside position, blocking, and passing. Many volleyball positions require similar skills, so these should be helpful beyond, for example, the outside hitter position. Based on the level of your athletes, the amount of time you have players in your sport, and level of play, you may adjust any of the following developmental sports scales to meet your specific needs.

Sample Prioritized Criteria for Volleyball Key Positions

→ Outside hitter attacking

→ Blocking

→ Passing

Outside Hitter Attacking Developmental Sports Scale Template

Sport: Volleyball		
Topic: Attacking From the Outside Position		
Level: High School		
3.0	**In addition to 2.0 knowledge and skills, the player demonstrates deeper applications and fluency with skills.** For example: • Adjusts approach to the ball based on the setter and opposing blockers (quicker as needed) • Arm swing powerful, with greater-than-average speed • Effectively attacks from any net position in the area • Wipes tips or attacks off the block	**Observations**
	2.5 Player exhibits all the score 2.0 components and some of the elite 3.0 components.	
2.0	**Expected player proficiencies** • Movement to ball efficient and purposeful • Arm swing generates power for the attack • Follow-through after ball contact for spin and power • Eyes track set for positioning on the net • Ability to attack various net and set positions • Ball contact open handed and solid • Ability to attack line or cross court, as situation warrants. • Tips ball effectively • Hits off speed effectively **The player exhibits no major errors or omissions.**	
	1.5 Player exhibits all the score 1.0 components and some of the 2.0 components.	

1.0	**Player knows and demonstrates basic knowledge and skills:**
	 • Recognizes or recalls specific sport terminology, such as—
	    → *ball contact*
	    → *spin*
	    → *tips*
	    → *off-speed hits*
	    → *line*
	    → *cross court*
	 Simpler knowledge and skills:
	 • Moves to ball inefficiently—too many steps and limited gather step
	 • Arm swing weak
	 • Limited follow-through after ball contact
	 • Eyes don't track set for positioning on the net
	 • Attacks only common set position
	 • Ball contact side of hand or weak
	 • Ability to attack cross court as situation warrants
	 • Tips ball ineffectively	

Blocking Developmental Sports Scale Template

Sport: Volleyball		
Topic: Blocking		
Level: High School		

3.0	**In addition to 2.0 knowledge and skills, the player demonstrates deeper applications and fluency with skills.**	**Observations**
	For example:	
	• Blocks from any front row position (outside, middle, or off side) effectively	
	• Efficient footwork to time with other blockers for one, two, or three blockers	
	• Strong power in directing block downward and into opposing court	
	• Adjusts timing for various sets	
	2.5 Player exhibits all the score 2.0 components and some of the elite 3.0 components.	
2.0	**Expected player proficiencies**	
	• Moves to ball efficiently and with purpose—slide or crossover steps	
	• Timing footwork and jump with other blockers	
	• Uses arms for power but stays out of net	
	• Arms reach overhead with a pike position, closing over net	
	• Hands strong and fingers spread wide	
	• Eyes track ball to hitter back to ball	
	• Times the jump to match the ball attack	
	• Uses soft block technique as appropriate	
	The player exhibits no major errors or omissions.	
	1.5 Player exhibits all the score 1.0 components and some of the 2.0 components.	
1.0	**Player knows and demonstrates basic knowledge and skills:**	
	• Recognizes or recalls specific sport terminology, such as—	
	→ *hands strong*	
	→ *pike position*	
	→ *soft block*	
	Simpler knowledge and skills:	
	• Moves to ball inefficiently, lacks drop off net and stutter steps the slide	
	• Lacks timing with other blockers—staggers jump	
	• Arms often bump net when moving	
	• Arms reach overhead but lack pike position without net closure	
	• Hands and fingers weak	
	• Eyes track ball but miss hitter arm before jumping	
	• Timing off in matching the ball attack from opposing hitter	

Passing Developmental Sports Scale Template

Sport: Volleyball		
Topic: Passing		
Level: High School		

3.0	**In addition to 2.0 knowledge and skills, the player demonstrates deeper applications and fluency with skills.** For example: • Adjusts arm angles for difficult serves • Absorbs hard-driven serves for softer pass • Adjusts receiving position based on server, angle, spin, or depth • Consistently passes to setter 90 percent or more of time	**Observations**
	2.5 Player exhibits all the score 2.0 components and some of the elite 3.0 components.	
2.0	**Expected player proficiencies** • Arm platform flat • Shoulders drop and angle toward setter (or direction of the pass) • Fingers loosely clasped or hands cupped for fast reception • Spin reduced off the arms • Calculates distance and height for next play • Positions self for various serves and servers **The player exhibits no major errors or omissions.**	
	1.5 Player exhibits all the score 1.0 components and some of the 2.0 components.	

1.0	**Player knows and demonstrates basic knowledge and skills:**
	
	• Recognizes or recalls specific sport terminology, such as—
	  → *arm platform*
	  → *shoulders drop*
	  → *distance and height calculated*
	
	Simpler knowledge and skills:
	
	• Arm platform staggered, causing some shanked passes
	• Shoulders don't drop and angle toward setter (or direction of the pass)
	• Fingers tightly clasped or hands not together for smooth transition or positioning
	• Ball spins off arms
	• Miscalculates distance (too far) or height for next play
	• Passes from a place instead of varying positioning based on serve types or servers	

Developmental Sports Scales for Intangibles

While coaches may include intangibles in developmental sports scales alongside knowledge and skills, sometimes it makes sense to assess them separately. Based on the level of your athletes, the amount of time you have players in your sport, and level of play, you may adjust any of the following developmental sports scales to meet your specific needs.

Sample Prioritized Criteria for Intangibles

→ Communication

→ Effort and attitude

→ Coachability

→ Hustle

→ Teamwork

Communication Developmental Sports Scale Template

Focus: Intangibles		
Topic: Communication		
Level: High School		
3.0	**In addition to 2.0 knowledge and skills, the player demonstrates deeper applications and fluency with skills.** For example: • Clearly articulates skill and behavioral requirements for the sport both verbally and in writing • Notices nonverbal behaviors from players and coaches and addresses issues of potential miscommunication quickly and directly with them • Notices when teammates need to express themselves and encourages them to do so, including suggesting appropriate times and places • Alerts coaches of potential issues regarding communication based on the pulse of practice, players' reactions, and the like	**Observations**
	2.5 Player exhibits all the score 2.0 components and some of the elite 3.0 components.	
2.0	**Expected player proficiencies** • Verbally articulates skill requirements for the sport • Addresses issues of potential miscommunication quickly and directly with players and coaches • Notices when teammates need to express themselves and encourages them to do so **The player exhibits no major errors or omissions.**	
	1.5 Player exhibits all the score 1.0 components and some of the 2.0 components.	
1.0	**Player knows and demonstrates basic knowledge and skills:** • Recognizes or recalls specific sport terminology, such as— → *articulates skill requirements* → *miscommunication* → *express oneself* **Simpler knowledge and skills:** • Verbally expresses some skills and knowledge for the sport, but struggles in some areas • Addresses issues of potential miscommunication indirectly with players and coaches behind their backs or through frustrating behaviors • May get frustrated when teammates need to express themselves	

Effort and Attitude Developmental Sports Scale Template

Focus: Intangibles			
Topic: Effort and Attitude			
Level: High School			
3.0	**In addition to 2.0 knowledge and skills, the player demonstrates deeper applications and fluency with skills.** For example: • Demonstrates team leadership and involvement exceeding expectations, such as organizing the team for practice, actively assisting other players to help them understand, and so on • Focuses on the task exceeding expectations, such as being self-directed and having an enthusiastic attitude • Prepares to learn exceeding expectations by arriving early to practice and consistently working hard • Exceeds deadlines and practice expectations by turning in reflections with honest and detailed information and holding self to a high standard		**Observations**
	2.5	Player exhibits all the score 2.0 components and some of the elite 3.0 components.	
2.0	**Expected player proficiencies** • Leads and is actively involved in practice situations and discussions by sharing information and sometimes even performing a leadership role • Focuses on the practice task by working independently, self-adjusting, and exhibiting a positive attitude • Prepares to learn by being on time, bringing proper equipment, and showing up ready to work hard • Meets deadlines and practice expectations **The player exhibits no major errors or omissions.**		
	1.5	Player exhibits all the score 1.0 components and some of the 2.0 components.	

1.0	**Player knows and demonstrates basic knowledge and skills:**
	• Recognizes or recalls specific sport terminology, such as—
	  → *leads during practice*
	  → *shows a positive attitude*
	  → *practice expectations*
	Simpler knowledge and skills:
	• Demonstrates reduced involvement in practice situations; requires prompts to participate, relies on the contributions of others, and struggles to initiate sharing information
	• Attends practice inconsistently; struggles to arrive on time, bring proper equipment, and be ready to work hard
	• Focuses on the task only with frequent reminders and relies on others to perform the drill or model techniques
	• Prepares to learn only with frequent reminders to be on time, bring equipment, and be ready to practice
	• Struggles to meet practice quality expectations, needing consistent reminders to review a skill and modify form
	• Demonstrates awareness of deadlines and practice quality expectations inconsistently; initiates arrangements with coach to address lateness or redo skills		

Developmental Sports Scales for Intangibles

Coachability Developmental Sports Scale Template

Focus: Intangibles		
Topic: Coachability		
Level: High School		

			Observations
3.0		**In addition to 2.0 knowledge and skills, the player demonstrates deeper applications and fluency with skills.** For example: • Quickly and effectively incorporates coaching feedback into practice and gameplay • Demonstrates a high level of receptiveness and adaptability to different coaching styles • Proactively seeks guidance and consistently asks insightful questions • Welcomes constructive criticism as an opportunity for growth and actively seeks feedback from coaches	
	2.5	Player exhibits all the score 2.0 components and some of the elite 3.0 components.	
2.0		**Expected player proficiencies** • Actively listens and consistently applies coaching instructions • Demonstrates a willingness to learn and improve performance • Seeks guidance and asks relevant questions to enhance understanding • Accepts constructive criticism with an open mind and uses it to make necessary adjustments **The player exhibits no major errors or omissions.**	
	1.5	Player exhibits all the score 1.0 components and some of the 2.0 components.	

Score 1.0		**Player knows and demonstrates basic knowledge and skills:**
		
		 • Recognizes or recalls specific sport terminology, such as—
		   → *adaptability*
		   → *guidance*
		   → *constructive criticism*
		
		 Simpler knowledge and skills:
		
		 • Struggles to implement feedback or follow instructions from coaches consistently
		 • Demonstrates resistance to change and displays a lack of adaptability
		 • Rarely seeks guidance or asks questions to clarify instructions
		 • Often exhibits a defensive attitude when receiving constructive criticism	

Hustle Developmental Sports Scale Template

Focus: Intangibles			
Topic: Hustle			
Level: High School			
3.0	**In addition to 2.0 knowledge and skills, the player demonstrates deeper applications and fluency with skills.**		**Observations**
	For example: • Demonstrates an unwavering commitment to hustling by consistently giving 100 percent effort in every practice and game, exceeding expectations • Serves as a catalyst for the team's energy and momentum, constantly motivating teammates and setting the example for hustle on and off the field • Displays a fearless attitude by diving for loose balls and putting in extra effort to make impactful plays		
	2.5	Player exhibits all the score 2.0 components and some of the elite 3.0 components.	
2.0	**Expected player proficiencies** • Demonstrates a reliable and consistent hustle in practices and games, always giving the best effort and consistently making plays that contribute to the team's success • Effectively communicates and encourages teammates to hustle, fostering a culture of high energy and effort throughout the team • Possesses the ability to recognize and seize opportunities through hustle, whether it's chasing down loose balls, making quick recoveries, or disrupting opponents' plays **The player exhibits no major errors or omissions.**		
	1.5	Player exhibits all the score 1.0 components and some of the 2.0 components.	

1.0	**Player knows and demonstrates basic knowledge and skills:**
	• Recognizes or recalls specific sport terminology, such as—
	   → *relentless*
	   → *reliable*
	   → *consistent*
	   → *high-energy*
	Simpler knowledge and skills:
	• Displays moments of hustle but struggles to maintain a consistent level of effort throughout practices and games, occasionally lacking the drive to go the extra mile
	• Needs to develop a greater awareness of hustle opportunities on the field and improve the instinct to actively seek out ways to contribute through hustle plays
	• Shows potential to develop a tenacious hustling mentality but requires further guidance and practice to fully embrace the hustle mindset		

Developmental Sports Scales for Intangibles

Teamwork Developmental Sports Scale Template

Focus: Intangibles		
Topic: Teamwork		
Level: High School		

3.0	**In addition to 2.0 knowledge and skills, the player demonstrates deeper applications and fluency with skills.**	Observations
	For example:	
	• Demonstrates a collaborative mindset by actively seeking opportunities to work with teammates, being willing to compromise, and valuing the contributions of others	
	• Acts as a reliable team player by consistently fulfilling team responsibilities, supporting and encouraging teammates, and exceeding expectations to ensure team success	
	• Practices adaptability by being flexible and adjusting to changes in circumstance, roles, and strategies for the benefit of the team	
2.5	Player exhibits all the score 2.0 components and some of the elite 3.0 components.	
2.0	**Expected player proficiencies**	
	• Demonstrates a cooperative attitude, is open to suggestions from teammates, and works well in group settings	
	• Consistently fulfills team responsibilities and regularly supports and encourages teammates	
	• Shows some degree of flexibility in adjusting to changing circumstances, roles, and strategies for the benefit of the team	
	The player exhibits no major errors or omissions.	
1.5	Player exhibits all the score 1.0 components and some of the 2.0 components.	
1.0	**Player knows and demonstrates basic knowledge and skills:**	
	• Recognizes or recalls specific sport terminology, such as—	
	→ *collaborative*	
	→ *compromise*	
	→ *adapting*	
	Simpler knowledge and skills:	
	• Demonstrates a developing willingness to collaborate with teammates but may occasionally struggle with compromising or recognizing the value of others' contributions	
	• Works toward fulfilling team responsibilities but may occasionally require reminders and support from teammates	
	• Shows effort in adapting to changing circumstances, roles, and strategies but may need further development in this area	

References and Resources

Active Network & Sporting Goods Manufacturers Association. (2012, Fall). *The journey of sports participation: 2012 grassroots sports participation in America study*. Washington, DC: Sporting Goods Manufacturers Association.

Ainsworth, L. (2003). *Power standards: Identifying the standards that matter the most*. Denver, CO: Advanced Learning Press.

Amorose, A. J., & Anderson-Butcher, D. (2007). Autonomy-supportive coaching and self-determined motivation in high school and college athletes: A test of self-determination theory. *Psychology of Sport and Exercise, 8*(5), 654–670.

Aspen Institute. (2020). *State of play 2020: Pandemic trends*. Accessed at www.aspenprojectplay.org/state-of-play-2020/pandemic-trends on May 22, 2023.

Aspen Institute. (n.d.a). *Fields of dreams: Innovate and they will come?* [Roundtable summary]. Washington, DC: Author. Accessed at https://static1.squarespace.com/static/595ea7d6e58c62dce01d1625/t/5a590121085229e4544b6c97/1515782435488/Fields+of+Dreams+Event+Summary.pdf on February 27, 2023.

Aspen Institute. (n.d.b). *Kid-focused, coach-driven: What training is needed?* [Roundtable summary]. Washington, DC: Author. Accessed at https://assets.aspeninstitute.org/wp-content/uploads/files/content/upload/Kid_Focused_Coach_Driven_Summary_Report.pdf on February 27, 2023.

Aspen Institute. (n.d.c). *Reimagining school sports: Large suburban public high schools*. Washington, DC: Author. Accessed at https://aspeninstitute.org/wp-content/uploads/2021/06/2021_Aspen_Suburban-Large-Report_updated2.pdf on June 30, 2022.

Aspen Institute. (n.d.d). *Sport for all, play for life: A playbook to develop every student through sports*. Washington, DC: Author. Accessed at https://aspeninstitute.org/wp-content/uploads/2022/02/FINAL-Aspen-Institute-Reimagining-School-Sports-playbook-pages.pdf on February 27, 2023.

Aspen Institute. (n.d.e). *Sport for all, play for life: A playbook to get every kid in the game*. Washington, DC: Author. Accessed at https://aspeninstitute.org/wp-content/uploads/2015/01/Aspen-Institute-Project-Play-Report.pdf on June 19, 2023.

Aspen Institute. (n.d.f). *What does the science say about athletic development in children?* Gainesville: University of Florida's Sport Policy & Research Collaborative. Accessed at https://assets.aspeninstitute.org/wp-content/uploads/2016/06/Project-play-september-2013-roundtable-research-brief.pdf on February 27, 2023.

Aspen Institute & Resonant Education. (2020–2021). *National student survey analysis: 2020–2021 administration.* Washington, DC: Aspen Institute. Accessed at https://aspeninstitute.org/wp-content/uploads/2021/11/Aspen-National-Student-Survey-FINAL-Report.pdf on February 27, 2023.

Balyi, I., & Hamilton, A. (1995). The concept of long-term athlete development. *Strength and Conditioning Coach, 3*(2), 5–6.

Bandura, A. (1977). *Social learning theory.* Prentice Hall.

Bangert-Drowns, R. L., Kulik, C.-L. C., Kulik, J. A., & Morgan, M. (1991). The instructional effect of feedback in test-like events. *Review of Educational Research, 61*(2), 213–238.

Barker, J. E., Semenov, A. D., Michaelson, L., Provan, L. S., Snyder, H. R., & Munakata, Y. (2014). Less-structured time in children's daily lives predicts self-directed executive functioning. *Frontiers in Psychology, 5,* 593.

Barnett, N. P., Smoll, F. L., & Smith, R. E. (1992). Effects of enhancing coach-athlete relationships on youth sport attrition. *The Sport Psychologist, 6*(2), 111–127.

Beatty, G., & Fawver, B. (n.d.). *What is the status of youth coach training in the U.S.?* Washington, DC: Aspen Institute. Accessed at https://aspeninstitute.org/wp-content/uploads/files/content/upload/Project%20Play%20Research%20Brief%20Coaching%20Education%20--%20FINAL.pdf on February 27, 2023.

Berk, R. A. (1986). A consumer's guide to setting performance standards on criterion-referenced tests. *Review of Educational Research, 56*(1), 137–172.

Berk, R. A. (1996). Standard setting: The next generation (where few psychometricians have gone before!). *Applied Measurement in Education, 9*(3), 215–225.

Bowlby, J. (1983). *Attachment: Attachment and loss* (Vol. 1). New York: Basic Books.

Brenner, J. S., (2016). Sports specialization and intensive training in young athletes. *Pediatrics, 138*(3), 2016–2148. https://doi.org/10.1542/peds.2016-2148

Brenner, J. S., LaBotz, M., Sugimoto, D., & Stracciolini, A. (2019). The psychosocial implications of sport specialization in pediatric athletes. *Journal of Athletic Training, 54*(10), 1021–1029.

Bronfenbrenner, U. (1979). *The ecology of human development: Experiments by nature and design.* Cambridge, MA: Harvard University Press.

Brookhart, S. M. (2008). *How to give effective feedback to your students.* Alexandria, VA: ASCD.

Brookhart, S. M. (2013). Classroom assessment in the context of motivation theory and research. In J. H. McMillan (Ed.), *SAGE handbook of research on classroom assessment* (pp. 35–54). Thousand Oaks, CA: SAGE.

Brookhart, S. M. (2017). *How to give effective feedback to your students* (2nd ed.). Alexandria, VA: ASCD.

Brown, S. M., & Walberg, H. J. (1993). Motivational effects on test scores of elementary students. *Journal of Educational Research, 86*(3), 133–136.

Buckendahl, C. W., Plake, B. S., & Impara, J. C. (2004). A strategy for evaluating district developed assessments for state accountability. *Educational Measurement: Issues and Practice, 23*(2), 17–25.

CareerExplorer. (n.d.). *The job market for physical education teachers in the United States.* Accessed at www.careerexplorer.com/careers/physical-education-teacher/job-market on May 25, 2023.

Carlson, R. (1993). The path to the national level in sports in Sweden. *Scandinavian Journal of Medicine and Science in Sports, 3*(3), 170–177.

Cavill, N., Kahlmeier, S., & Racioppi, F. (2006). *Physical activity and health in Europe: Evidence for action.* Copenhagen, Denmark: WHO Regional Office for Europe. Accessed at https://apps.who.int/iris/handle/10665/328052 on October 20, 2022.

Conley, B. (2008, July 22). *The importance of intangibles in recruiting.* Accessed at https://espn.com/collegesports/recruiting/football/columns/story?columnist=conley_bill&id=3499947 on June 4, 2023.

Côté, J. (1999). The influence of the family in the development of talent in sport. *The Sport Psychologist, 13*(4), 395–417.

Curran, T., Hill, A. P., Hall, H. K., & Jowett, G. E. (2015). Relationships between the coach-created motivational climate and athlete engagement in youth sport. *Journal of Sport and Exercise Psychology, 37*(2), 193–198. https://doi.org/10.1123/jsep.2014-0203

Deci, E. L., & Ryan, R. M. (1985). *Intrinsic motivation and self-determination in human behavior.* New York: Plenum Press.

Deci, E. L., & Ryan, R. M. (2008). Self-determination theory: A macrotheory of human motivation, development, and health. *Canadian Psychology, 49*(3), 182–185. https://doi.org/10.1037/a0012801

Doran, G. T. (1981). There's a S.M.A.R.T way to write management's goals and objectives. *Management Review, 70*(11), 35–36.

Duda, J. L. (1989). Relationship between task and ego orientation and the perceived purpose of sport among high school athletes. *Journal of Sport and Exercise Psychology, 11*(3), 318–335. Accessed at https://journals.humankinetics.com/view/journals/jsep/11/3/article-p318.xml on August 19, 2022.

Duffy, P., Hartley, H., Bales, J., Crespo, M., Dick, F., Vardhan, D. et al. (2011). Sport coaching as a "profession": Challenges and future directions. *International Journal of Sports Science and Coaching, 5*(2), 93–123.

Dunn, C. R., Dorsch, T. E., King, M. Q., & Rothlisberger, K. J. (2016). The impact of family financial investment on perceived parent pressure and child enjoyment and commitment in organized youth sport. *Family Relations: Interdisciplinary Journal of Applied Family Studies, 65*(2), 287–299.

Epstein, D. (2014, June 10). Sports should be child's play. *The New York Times*, p. A23.

Erikson, E. H. (1950). *Childhood and society.* New York: Norton.

Farrey, T. (2008). *Game on: The all-American race to make champions of our children.* New York: ESPN Books.

Fisher, D., & Frey, N. (2012). Making time for feedback. *Educational Leadership, 70*(1). Accessed at www.ascd.org/el/articles/making-time-for-feedback on August 26, 2022.

Flygare, J., Hoegh, J. K., & Heflebower, T. (2022). *Planning and teaching in the standards-based classroom.* Bloomington, IN: Marzano Resources.

Fuhrman, S. H., & Elmore, R. F. (Eds.). (2004). *Redesigning accountability systems for education* [Consortium for Policy Research in Education Policy Briefs]. New York: Teachers College Press. Accessed at http://untag-smd.ac.id/files/Perpustakaan_Digital_1/ACCOUNTABILITY%20Redesigning%20accountability%20systems%20for%20education.pdf on June 12, 2023.

Gessel, L. M., Fields, S. K., Collins, C. L., Dick, R. W., & Comstock, R. D. (2007). Concussions among United States high school and collegiate athletes. *Journal of Athletic Training, 42*(4), 495–503.

Gill, D. L., Gross, J. B., & Huddleston, S. (1983). Participation motivation in youth sports. *International Journal of Sport Psychology, 14*(1), 1–14.

Gladwell, M. (2000). *The tipping point: How little things can make a big difference.* Boston: Little, Brown.

Goodreads. (n.d.). *Thomas Colley quotes.* Accessed at www.goodreads.com/quotes/112837-i-am-not-who-you-think-i-am-i-am on February 28, 2023.

Graham, R., Rivara, F. P., Ford, M. A., & Mason Spicer, C. (Eds.). (2014). *Sports-related concussions in youth: Improving the science, changing the culture.* Washington, DC: The National Academies Press.

Gregory, S. (2017, August 24). How kids' sports became a $15 billion industry. *TIME.* Accessed at https://time.com/magazine/us/4913681/september-4th-2017-vol-190-no-9-u-s on February 27, 2023.

Guskey, T. R. (1994). Making the grade: What benefits students? *Educational Leadership, 52*(2), 14–20.

Hattie, J. (2009). *Visible learning: A synthesis of over 800 meta-analyses relating to achievement.* New York: Routledge.

Heflebower, T. (2005). *An educator's perception of STARS from selected Nebraska education service unit staff developers* [Unpublished doctoral dissertation, University of Nebraska–Lincoln]. Digital Commons. Accessed at https://digitalcommons.unl.edu/dissertations/AAI3194116 on August 28, 2023.

Heflebower, T., with Hoegh, J. K. (2020). *Crafting your message: Tips and tricks for educators to deliver perfect presentations.* Bloomington, IN: Solution Tree Press.

Heflebower, T., Hoegh, J. K., & Warrick, P. B. (2014). *A school leader's guide to standards-based grading.* Bloomington, IN: Marzano Resources.

Heflebower, T., Hoegh, J. K., & Warrick, P. B. (2021). *Leading standards-based learning: An implementation guide for schools and districts.* Bloomington, IN: Marzano Resources.

Heflebower, T., Hoegh, J. K., Warrick, P. B., & Flygare, J. (2019). *A teacher's guide to standards-based learning.* Bloomington, IN: Marzano Resources.

Hoegh, J. K., with Heflebower, T., & Warrick, P. B. (2020). *A handbook for developing and using proficiency scales in the classroom.* Bloomington, IN: Marzano Resources.

Hoegh, J. K., Flygare, J., Heflebower, T., & Warrick, P. B. (2023). *Assessing learning in the standards-based classroom: A practical guide for teachers.* Bloomington, IN: Marzano Resources.

Hospital for Special Surgery. (n.d.). *Intensive participation in a single sport: Good or bad for kids?* Accessed at www.hss.edu/pediatrics-intensive-participation-single-sport-good-bad-kids.asp on February 1, 2022.

Impara, J. C., & Plake, B. S. (1997). Standard setting: An alternative approach. *Journal of Educational Measurement, 34*(4), 353–366.

International Council for Coaching Excellence & Association of Summer Olympic International Federations. (2012). *International sport coaching framework* (version 1.1). Champaign, IL: Human Kinetics. Accessed at https://icce.ws/wp-content/uploads/2023/01/ISCF_1_aug_2012.pdf on June 5, 2023.

International Council for Coaching Excellence, Association of Summer Olympic International Federations, & Leeds Metropolitan University. (2013). *International sport coaching framework* (version 1.2). Champaign, IL: Human Kinetics.

Iwasaki, S., Fry, M. D., & Hogue, C. M. (2021). Mindful engagement mediates the relationship between motivational climate perceptions and coachability for male high school athletes. *Journal of Clinical Sport Psychology, 16*(3), 234–253. https://doi.org/10.1123/jcsp.2020–0016

Joshua. (2019, May 9). *The three intangibles of athletics.* Accessed at www.coachup.com/nation/articles/the-3-intangibles-of-athletics# on June 5, 2023.

Koltko-Rivera, M. E. (2006). Rediscovering the later version of Maslow's hierarchy of needs: Self-transcendence and opportunities for theory, research, and unification. *Review of General Psychology, 10*(4), 302–317.

Kristensen, A. H., Flottemesch, T. J., Maciosek, M. V., Jenson, J., Barclay, G., Ashe, M., et al. (2014). Reducing childhood obesity through U.S. federal policy. *American Journal of Preventative Medicine, 47*(5), 604–612.

Lee, A. (2015, February 24). *Seven charts that show the state of youth sports in the US and why it matters* [Blog post]. Accessed at www.aspeninstitute.org/blog-posts/7-charts-that-show-the-state-of-youth-sports-in-the-us-and-why-it-matters on June 6, 2023.

Locke, E. A., & Latham, G. P. (1990). *A theory of goal setting and task performance.* Hoboken, NJ: Prentice Hall.

Lyle, J. (2002). *Sport coaching concepts: A framework for coaches' behaviour.* London: Routledge.

Marzano, R. J. (2003). *What works in schools: Translating research into action.* Alexandria, VA: ASCD.

Marzano, R. J. (2006). *Classroom assessment and grading that work.* Alexandria, VA: ASCD.

Marzano, R. J. (2009). *Designing and teaching learning goals and objectives.* Bloomington, IN: Marzano Resources.

Marzano, R. J. (2010). *Formative assessment and standards-based grading.* Bloomington, IN: Marzano Resources.

Marzano, R. J. (2017). *The new art and science of teaching.* Bloomington, IN: Solution Tree Press.

Marzano, R. J., Norford, J. S., Finn, M., & Finn, D., III. (2017). *A handbook for personalized competency-based education.* Bloomington, IN: Marzano Resources.

Marzano, R. J., Yanoski, D. C., with Paynter, D. E. (2016). *Proficiency scales for the new science standards: A framework for science instruction and assessment.* Bloomington, IN: Marzano Resources.

Maslow, A. H. (1943). A theory of human motivation. *Psychological Review, 50*(4), 370–396.

Maslow, A. H. (1954). *Motivation and personality.* New York: Harper & Row.

Maslow, A. H. (1969). The farther reaches of human nature. *Journal of Transpersonal Psychology, 1*(1), 1–9.

Maslow, A. H. (1979). *The journals of A. H. Maslow* (R. J. Lowry, Ed., Vols. 1–2). Monterey, CA: Brooks/Cole.

Messner, M. A., & Musto, M. (2014). Where are the kids? *Sociology of Sport Journal, 31*(1), 102–122.

Miller, G. (2012). *Intangibles: Big-league stories and strategies for winning the mental game—in baseball and in life.* Ashland, OR: Byte Level Books.

Monteiro, D., Borrego, C. C., Silva, C., Moutão, J., Marinho, D. A., & Cid, L. (2018). Motivational climate sport youth scale: Measurement invariance across gender and five different sports. *Journal of Human Kinetics, 61*, 249–261. https://doi.org /10.1515/hukin-2017-0124

Moore, L. V., Roux, A. V. D., Evenson, K. R., McGinn, A. P., & Brines, S. J. (2008). Availability of recreational resources in minority and low socioeconomic status areas. *American Journal of Preventive Medicine, 34*(1), 16–22.

Moss, C. M., & Brookhart, S. M. (2009). *Advancing formative assessment in every classroom: A guide for instructional leaders.* Alexandria, VA: ASCD.

Nortje, A. (2021, May 3). *Piaget's stages: Four stages of cognitive development and theory.* Accessed at https://positivepsychology.com /piaget-stages-theory on February 27, 2023.

Ogden, C. L., Carroll, M. D., & Flegal, K. M. (2008). High body mass index for age among US children and adolescents, 2003–2006. *The Journal of the American Medical Association, 299*(20), 2401–2405.

Olympiou, A., Jowett, S., & Duda, J. L. (2008). The psychological interface between the coach-created motivational climate and the coach-athlete relationship in team sports. *The Sport Psychologist, 22*(4), 423–438. Accessed at https://journals .humankinetics.com/view/journals/tsp/22/4/article-p423.xml on August 19, 2022.

Papalia, D. E., & Feldman, R. D. (2011). *A child's world: Infancy through adolescence* (12th ed.). New York: McGraw-Hill.

Pekel, K., Roehlkepartain, E. C., Syvertsen, A. K., & Scales, P. C. (2015). *Don't forget the families: The missing piece in America's effort to help all children succeed.* Minneapolis, MN: Search Institute.

Piaget, J. (1951). *Play, dreams, and imitation in childhood.* London: Heinemann.

Popham, W. J. (2003). *Test better, teach better: The instructional role of assessment.* Alexandria, VA: ASCD.

Post, E. G., Trigsted, S. M., Riekena, J. W., Hetzel, S., McGuine, T. A., Brooks, M. A., et al. (2017). The association of sport specialization and training volume with injury history in youth athletes. *The American Journal of Sports Medicine, 45*(6), 1405–1412. https://doi:10.1177/0363546517690848

Reinboth, M., & Duda, J. L. (2004). The motivational climate, perceived ability, and athletes' psychological and physical well-being. *The Sport Psychologist, 18*(3), 237–251. Accessed at https://journals.humankinetics.com/view/journals/tsp/18/3/article -p237.xml on August 19, 2022.

Rottensteiner, C., Konttinen, N., & Laakso, L. (2015). Sustained participation in youth sports related to coach-athlete relationship and coach-created motivational climate. *International Sport Coaching Journal, 2*(1), 29–38. Accessed at https://journals .humankinetics.com/view/journals/iscj/2/1/article-p29.xml on August 19, 2022.

Ryan, R. M., & Deci, E. L. (2009). Promoting self-determined school engagement: Motivation, learning, and well-being. In K. R. Wentzel & A. Wigfield (Eds.), *Handbook of Motivation at School* (pp. 171–195). New York: Routledge.

Ryan, R. M., Williams, G. C., Patrick, H., & Deci, E. L. (2009). Self-determination theory and physical activity: The dynamics of motivation in development and wellness. *Hellenic Journal of Psychology, 6*(2), 107–124.

Sabo, D., & Veliz, P. (2008, October). *Go out and play: Youth sports in America.* East Meadow, NY: Women's Sports Foundation. Accessed at www.womenssportsfoundation.org/wp-content/uploads/2016/08/go_out_and_play_exec.pdf on February 27, 2023.

Saffici, C. (2015, March 10). Teaching and coaching: The challenges and conflicts of dual roles. *The Sport Journal.* Accessed at https://thesportjournal.org/article/teaching-coaching-the-challenges-and-conflicts-of-dual-roles on September 29, 2022.

Scales, P. C. (2016, May 1). The crucial coaching relationship. *Phi Delta Kappan, 97*(8), 19–23. Accessed at https://kappanonline .org/scales-crucial-coaching-relationship-students-sports on May 25, 2023.

Scholarship Stats.com. (n.d.). *Varsity odds.* Accessed at https://scholarshipstats.com/varsityodds on May 22, 2023.

Seefeldt, V., & Haubenstricker, J. (1982). Patterns, phases, or stages: An analytical model for the study of developmental movement. In J. A. S. Kelso & J. E. Clark (Eds.), *The development of movement control and coordination* (pp. 309–318). New York: Wiley.

Smoll, F. L., Smith, R. E., & Cumming, S. P. (2007). Effects of a motivational climate intervention for coaches on young athletes' achievement goal orientations. *Journal of Clinical Sport Psychology, 1*(1), 23–46. https://doi.org/10.1123/jcsp.1.1.23

Solomon, J. (2023, May 19). *Project Play Summit recap: Olympic reform panel explores big changes.* Accessed at www.aspenprojectplay .org/news?author=5e2f378710cbf81e7985b843 on June 6, 2023.

Solutions Research Group Consultants. (2014, June 10). *Massive competition in pursuit of the $5.7 billion Canadian youth sports market.* Accessed at www.srgnet.com/2014/06/10/massive-competition-in-pursuit-of-the-5-7-billion-canadian-youth-sports -market on May 22, 2023.

South African Sports Confederation and Olympic Committee. (2010). *The South African coaching framework: Declaration from the minister of sport and recreation and the president of South African Sports Confederation and Olympic Committee.* Johannesburg, South Africa: Author. Accessed at https://sasca-pb.co.za/wp-content/uploads/2020/04/SACF-Book-1.pdf on June 6, 2023.

Sports & Fitness Industry Association. (2021, December 21). *SFIA releases 2021 U.S. trends in team sports report.* Accessed at https://sfia.org/resources/sfia-releases-2021-us-trends-in-team-sports-repor on June 6, 2023.

Sporting Goods Manufacturers Association. (2012). *2012 sports, fitness and leisure activities topline participation report.* Accessed at http://assets.usta.com/assets/1/15/SGMA_Research_2012_Participation_Topline_Report.pdf. on May 6, 2023.

Stronge, J. H. (2018). *Qualities of effective teachers* (3rd ed.). Alexandria, VA: ASCD.

Troiano, R. P., Berrigan, D., Dodd, K. W., Mâsse, L. C., Tilert, T., & McDowell, M. (2008). Physical activity in the United States measured by accelerometer. *Medicine and Science in Sports and Exercise, 40*(1), 181–188.

USA Hockey's American Development Model. (n.d.). *What is the American development model?* Accessed at www.admkids.com on May 6, 2023.

Visek, A. J., Achrati, S. M., Mannix, H., McDonnell, K., Harris, B. S., & DiPietro, L. (2015). The fun integration theory: Toward sustaining children and adolescents sport participation. *Journal of Physical Activity and Health, 12*(3), 424–433.

Vossekuil, B. (n.d.). *Twenty team building exercises for youth sports.* Accessed at https://signupgenius.com/sports/team-building -sports.cfm on June 6, 2023.

Waite-Stupiansky, S. (2017). Jean Piaget's constructivist theory of learning. In L. E. Cohen & S. Waite-Stupiansky (Eds.), *Theories of early childhood education: Developmental, behaviorist, and critical* (pp. 3–17). New York: Routledge.

Whitehead, J. (2014, October 28). *Safety in youth sports: Parents have spoken, we have listened, and now we have to act.* Accessed at https://aspenprojectplay.org/news/2014/10/28/safety-in-youth-sports-parents-have-spoken-we-have-listened-and-now-we-have -to-act on February 27, 2023.

Wiliam, D. (2018). *Embedded formative assessment* (2nd ed.). Bloomington, IN: Solution Tree Press.

Wolf, K. P. (1993). From informal to informed assessment: Recognizing the role of the classroom teacher. *Journal of Reading, 36*(7), 518–523.

Women's Sports Foundation. (n.d.). *Issues related to girls and boys competing with and against each other in sports and physical activity settings.* Accessed at https://womenssportsfoundation.org/wp-content/uploads/2019/08/issues-related-to-girls-and-boys -competing-with-and-against-each-other-in-sports-and-physical-activity-settings-the-foundation-position.pdf on June 6, 2023.

World Health Organization & Food and Agriculture Organization of the United Nations. (2003). *Diet, nutrition and the prevention of chronic diseases.* Geneva, Switzerland: World Health Organization. Accessed at http://apps.who.int/iris/bitstream /handle/10665/42665/WHO_TRS_916.pdf;jsessionid=D12226AE4029D2B4C7B8159789E91A72?sequence=1 on February 28, 2023.

Index

A

activities for team building
    about, 45–46
    life boxes, 47
    note card notice, 46
    relic bags, 46–47
annual costs for families participating in sports, 4
Aspen Institute, 8, 27, 41
assistant coaches, roles and responsibilities of, 19–20.
    See also coaching
athlete maturation level, 13–15
attitude, 7, 54, 57, 83. *See also* intangibles
autonomy, 34, 41, 43

B

baseball. *See also* collegiate case study; high school
    experiential vignette
    developmental sports scales for, 117
    example developmental sports scale assessing glove
        positioning and ball tracking, 63
    example developmental sports scale assessing position
        and making plays, 64
    example developmental sports scale for positioning and
        making plays, 108
    reproducible developmental sports scales for, 118–120

basketball
    developmental sports scales for, 121
    reproducible developmental sports scales for, 122–124
belonging, 32, 33. *See also* Maslow's hierarchy of needs
Brookhart, S., 88, 89, 92

C

case study and experiential vignette of Coach Heflebower's players
    collegiate case study, 97–106
    high school experiential vignette, 107–112
    summary, 112
child-development models
    about, 28
    athlete maturation level and, 13–15
    Deci and Ryan's self-determination theory, 34–35
    Maslow's hierarchy of needs, 32–33
    Piaget's theory of cognitive development, 30
coaches, role of, 2
coaching
    coaching challenges, 2–3
    cycle of coaching, 17
    digital age and, 113
    establishing coaching roles and expectations. *See* roles
        and expectations
    fostering positive player-coach relationships. *See* player-coach
        relationships

implications for coaches, 36–42

proficiency-based coaching, 52–54. *See also* expectations
    for proficiency-based coaching

sport coaching defined, 11–12

tools for effective coaching, 7–8

coaching competencies, reproducible for, 23–25

coach-teachers, role of, 2

collegiate case study

    about, 97–98

    discussion, 106

    findings, 99–106

    method, 98–99

communication

    characteristics of successful coaches and, 15

    intangibles and, 57

    reproducibles for, 148

competitions, 16

concrete operational stage, 30. *See also* theory of cognitive
    development

Conley, B., 54–55

connection to something greater than self, 32, 33. *See also*
    Maslow's hierarchy of needs

"Crucial Coaching Relationship, The" (Scales), 43

D

determining what you will teach and assess. *See* expectations for
    proficiency-based coaching

developmental relationships, 43. *See also* player-coach
    relationships

developmental sports scales

    about, 58–59

    about using for tracking, feedback, and goal setting, 75

    benefits of using, 70

    customized developmental sports scales, 61–62, 65

    examples of, 63, 64, 108, 109

    feedback, characteristics of quality, 88–90

    goal setting and, 91–94

    practice session planning and, 67–68

    progress tracking and, 79, 81–83

    reflection practices and, 85–87

    reflections for, 60, 66, 69, 71, 78–79, 84, 87, 90–91, 94–95

    reproducibles for, 96, 116. *See also specific sports*

    role of in player development, 68

    sample customized template, 61

    sample including player self-assessment, 80

    sample script for introducing developmental sports scales
       to players, 76

    sample using highlighting, 81–82

    summary, 95

    team expectations and, 75–76, 78

    use of term, 53

E

essential skills. *See also* priority knowledge/skills

    collegiate case study and, 99, 100, 104

    feedback and, 89

    high school experiential vignette and, 107

    preassessments and, 67

establishing coaching roles and expectations. *See* roles and
    expectations

esteem within a community, 32, 33. *See also* Maslow's hierarchy
    of needs

expectations for proficiency-based coaching

    about, 51

    developmental sports scales and, 58–71

    generic form of a proficiency scale, 53

    priority knowledge, skills, and intangibles, 54–58

    proficiency-based coaching, 52–54

    reflections for, 53–54, 58, 60, 66, 69, 71

    reproducibles for, 73

    summary, 72

extrinsic motivation, 34, 41, 87. *See also* intrinsic motivation

F

family commitments and demographics

    about, 3

    financial and time commitments, 3–5

    physical and emotional strains, 5

feedback

    characteristics of quality feedback, 88–90

    coaches/coaching and, 2, 16, 52

    collegiate case study and, 98–99, 100, 101, 102, 103–105, 106

    developmental sports scales and, 68, 81–82

    goal setting and, 91, 92

    high school experiential vignette and, 111

    motivating players and, 41

    practice cycle and, 37–38

    practice session planning and, 67

    priority skills and, 57

    procedures to obtain player reflection and provide feedback, 78

    reflections for, 90–91

    sample two-week practice plan with embedded reflection and
       feedback, 85

    sample two-week preseason practice plan with multiple practices
       per day with embedded reflection and feedback, 86

financial and time commitments of families in sports, 3–5

Flygare, J., 52

football

    developmental sports scales for, 125

    reproducible developmental sports scales for, 126–128

formal operational stage, 30. *See also* theory of cognitive
    development

fostering positive player-coach relationships. *See* player-coach
    relationships

G

goals. *See also* SMART goals
  characteristics of successful coaches, 16–17
  collegiate case study and, 98–99, 100–101, 102, 103–106
  developmental sports scales and, 70
  feedback and, 88, 90
  goal setting, 91–92, 94
  motivation and, 35, 41
  reflections for, 94–95
  setting the vision and, 15
Gregory, S., 3

H

head coaches, roles and responsibilities of, 19–20.
    See also coaching
Heflebower, T., 52
Heflebower's players, case study and experiential vignette
    of coach. *See* case study and experiential vignette of
    Coach Heflebower's players
high school experiential vignette
  about, 107
  background, 107, 110
  example developmental sports scale for, 108, 109
  reflections, 111–112
  scenario for player one, 110
  scenario for player two, 110–111
Hoegh, J., 52, 88
"How Kids' Sports Became a $15 Billion Industry" (Gregory), 3

I

impartial competitions, 16
implications for coaches. *See also* coaching
  about, 36
  considering players' needs, 39
  implementing the practice cycle, 36–38
  motivating players from the inside out, 41–42
  reflections for, 40, 42
intangibles
  criteria for identifying, 55
  developmental sports scales for, 147
  matrix for identifying, 56
  priority knowledge, skills, and intangibles, 54–58
  reproducible developmental sports scales for, 148–152
  tools for effective coaching, 7
*Intangibles: Big-League Stories and Strategies for Winning the
    Mental Game—in Baseball and in Life* (Miller), 7
International Council for Coaching Excellence and the
    Association of Summer Olympic International
    Federation, 2–3, 12, 13, 19
intrinsic motivation. *See also* extrinsic motivation
  developmental sports scales and, 70, 111
  feedback and, 89
  motivating players and, 41
  player-coach relationships and, 43

progress tracking and, 79
  reflections and, 87
  self-determination theory and, 34
introduction
  about this book, 8–9
  coaching challenges, 2–3
  family commitments and demographics, 3–5
  impact of sports, 1–2
  pandemic impact, 6–7
  tools for effective coaching, 7–8

L

life boxes, 47
long-term athlete development, 14
long-term goals, 70. *See also* goals

M

Maslow's hierarchy of needs
  child-development models and, 32–33
  considering players' needs and, 39
  reflections for, 33–34
Miller, G., 7
modeling
  characteristics of successful coaches and, 13, 15
  goal setting and, 91
  practice cycle and, 37
monitoring/evaluating outcomes. *See* progress tracking
Moss, C., 92
motivating players from the inside out, 41–42. *See also* extrinsic
    motivation; intrinsic motivation

N

note card notice, 46

P

pandemic impact on sports, 6–7
participation and preparedness. *See also* intangibles
  example developmental sports scale for expectations for, 109
  reproducible developmental sports scales for, 149
  team expectations and, 77
physical education teachers, job growth in, 2
physiology, 32. *See also* Maslow's hierarchy of needs
Piaget, J. *See* theory of cognitive development
Planning and Teaching in the Standards-Based Classrooms (Flygare,
    Hoegh, and Heflebower), 52
player reflections, 78. *See also* reflection practices
player-coach relationships
  about, 27–28
  activities for team building, 45–47
  child-development models and, 28–36
  coaching roles and expectations and, 11, 15
  implications for coaches and, 36–42
  reflections for, 29, 31, 33–34, 35–36, 38–39, 40, 42,
      44–45, 47–48

reproducibles for, 49
successful player-coach relationships, 43–44
summary, 48
practice
conducting effective practices, 15–16
practice cycle, 36–39, 49
practice session planning, 67–69, 73
preassessments, 67
preoperational stage, 30. *See also* theory of cognitive development
priority knowledge/skills. *See also* essential skills
criteria for identifying, 55
developmental sports scales and, 58–59
expectations for proficiency-based coaching and, 54–58
reflections for, 58
proficiency-based coaching, 52–54. *See also* expectations for
proficiency-based coaching
progress tracking
athletic team tracking form, 83
coaching roles and expectations and, 16, 19–20
developmental sports scales and, 79, 81–83
practice cycle and, 37
reflections for, 84

R

reflection practices
developmental sports scales and, 85–87
procedures to obtain player reflection and provide feedback, 78
reflections for, 87
sample two-week practice plan with embedded reflection
and feedback, 85
sample two-week preseason practice plan with multiple practices
per day with embedded reflection and feedback, 86
relationships. *See* player-coach relationships
relic bag, 46–47
reproducibles for
developmental sports scales for baseball, 118–120
developmental sports scales for basketball, 122–124
developmental sports scales for football, 126–128
developmental sports scales for intangibles, 148–152
developmental sports scales for soccer, 134–138
developmental sports scales for softball, 130–132
developmental sports scales for track and field, 140–142
developmental sports scales for volleyball, 144–146
evaluating my coaching competencies, 23–25
implementing the practice cycle, 49
planning practice sessions, 73
sample developmental sports scale template, 116
setting SMART goals, 96
rival teams, 13, 16
roles and expectations
about, 11
characteristics of successful coaches, 13–18
coaching roles and expectations, 19–21
reflections for, 12, 18–19, 21–22
reproducibles for, 23–25

sport coaching defined, 11–12
summary, 22
Ryan, R., 34–35

S

safety, 32. *See also* Maslow's hierarchy of needs
Saffici, C., 2
Scales, P., 43
self-actualization, 32, 33. *See also* Maslow's hierarchy of needs
self-assessment
collegiate case study and, 98, 102, 105, 106
developmental sports scales and, 67, 81, 82
esteem within a community and, 33
priority skills and, 57
proficiency-based coaching and, 52
sample developmental sports scale including player self-
assessment, 80
self-determination theory (SDT)
child-development models and, 34–35
motivating players from the inside out and, 41–42
reflections for, 35–36
sensorimotor stage, 30. *See also* theory of cognitive development
SMART goals. *See also* goals
goal setting and, 92
reproducibles for, 96
template for setting SMART goals, 93
soccer
developmental sports scales for, 133
reproducible developmental sports scales for, 134–138
softball
developmental sports scales for, 129
reproducible developmental sports scales for, 130–132
sports
annual costs for families participating in sports, 4
impact of, 1–2, 7
pandemic impact on, 6–7
sport coaching defined, 11–12

T

teacher-coaches, role of, 2
teachers, role of, 2
teaching, 37, 67
team building. *See* activities for team building
team expectations
developmental sports scales and, 75–76, 78
expectations for participation and preparedness, 77
reflections for, 78–79
teamwork. *See also* intangibles
on athletic tracking form, 83
feedback and, 90
reproducibles for, 152
theory of cognitive development
child-development models and, 30
practice cycle and, 36
reflections for, 31

tough love, 11
track and field
    developmental sports scales for, 139
    reproducible developmental sports scales for, 140–142

U

University of Florida Sport Policy and Research Collaborative, 44
using developmental sports scales for tracking, feedback, and goal
    setting. *See* developmental sports scales

V

vision, 15, 35
volleyball
    developmental sports scales for, 143
    reproducible developmental sports scales for, 144–146
volunteer coaches, roles and responsibilities of, 19–20. *See also*
    coaching

W

Wiliam, D., 89

Planning and Teaching in the Standards-Based Classroom
Jeff Flygare, Jan K. Hoegh, and Tammy Heflebower
Shifting to standards-based learning is a big change. Rely on *Planning and Teaching in the Standards-Based Classroom* to help you move forward with clarity and confidence. This can't-miss guide delivers straightforward, practical tools and detailed instructions for everything from lesson planning to proficiency scales to parent communication.
BKL069

A Teacher's Guide to Standards-Based Learning
Tammy Heflebower, Jan K. Hoegh, Philip B. Warrick, and Jeff Flygare
Designed specifically for K–12 teachers, this guide provides a sequential approach to implementing standards-based education in the classroom. Transition to more effective instructional strategies and use standards-based grading and assessment methods to better measure student learning.
BKL044

Bolstering Student Resilience
Jason E. Harlacher and Sara A. Whitcomb
Move beyond the buzzwords surrounding social-emotional learning and focus on three fundamentals for successfully supporting your students. This book illuminates the why behind the work and offers proven strategies for building positive, supportive classrooms.
BKL063

Motivating and Inspiring Students
Robert J. Marzano, Darrell Scott, Tina H. Boogren, and Ming Lee Newcomb
Discover a results-driven framework—based on a six-level hierarchy of student needs and goals—that you can use to provide engaging instruction to students.
BKL025

A Handbook for Developing and Using Proficiency Scales in the Classroom
Jan K. Hoegh
Discover a clear path for creating and utilizing high-quality proficiency scales. Through this practical handbook, you will gain access to a comprehensive toolkit of strategies, methods, and examples for a variety of content areas and grade levels.
BKL045

Solution Tree | Press a division of
Solution Tree

Visit solution-tree.com or call 800.733.6786 to order.

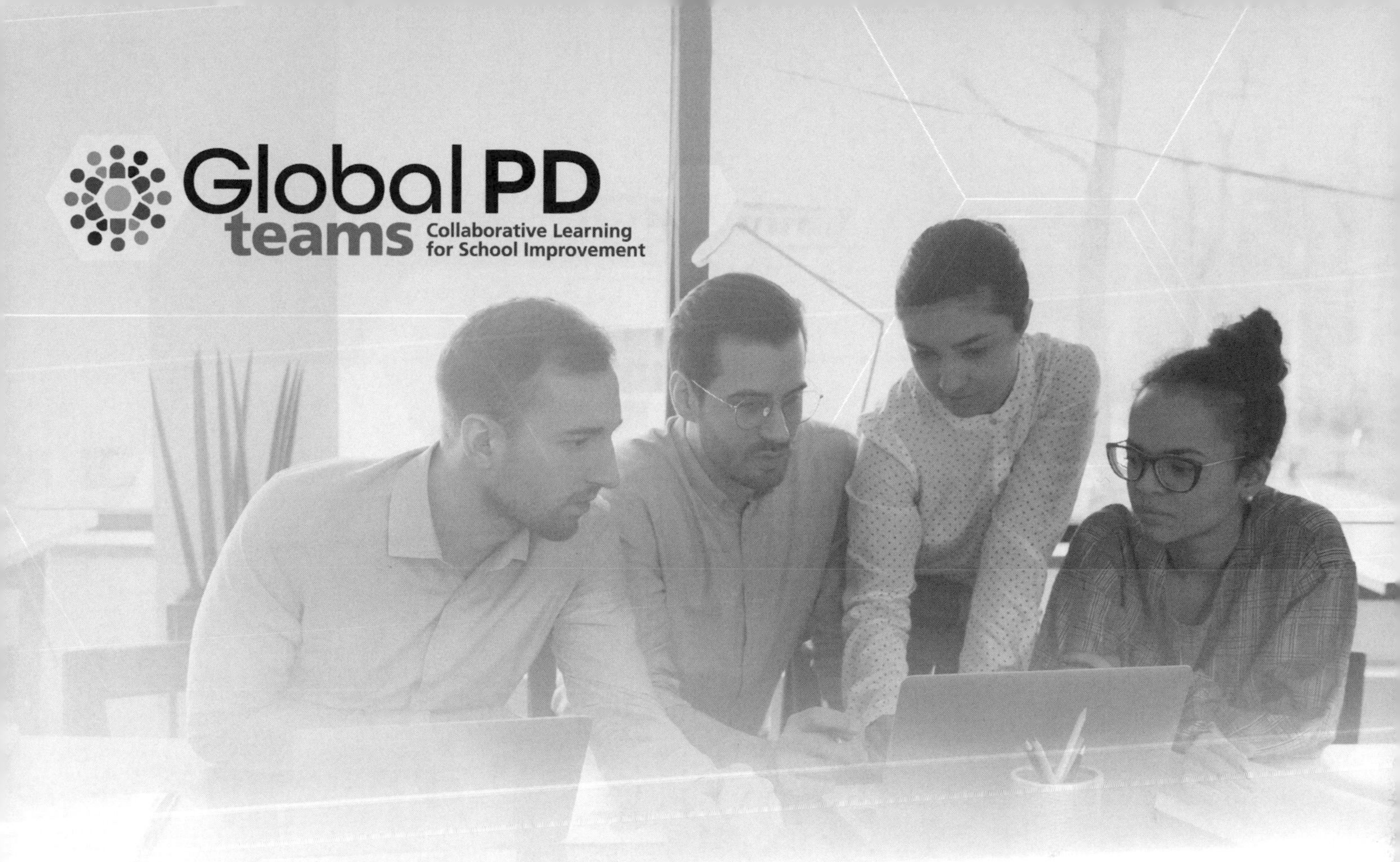